The Windies' City
Chicago's Historical Hidden Treasures

Greg Borzo, Suzanne Haynes and Bernard Turner

The Windies' City
Chicago's Historical Hidden Treasures

Highlights of Chicago Press
Publishing for Chicago's History and Culture

Other books from Highlights of Chicago Press:
A View of Bronzeville
TJ and the Mysterious Stranger
Our Chicago—People and Places

For information address: Highlights of Chicago Press, 4325 N. Central Park Ave., Chicago, IL 60618-1022

ISBN: 978-0-9710487-3-7
First Edition

Book layout and design by Ok To Dream, LLC™, P.O. Box 595, Conyers, GA 30013 www.ok2dream.net

HIGHLIGHTS OF CHICAGO

The Windies' City
Chicago's Historical Hidden Treasures

Introduction

By Gary T. Johnson, President, Chicago History Museum

A funny thing happened on my way to becoming a Chicago History Museum volunteer – they made me President. During my 28 years of practicing law in Chicago, more and more of my weekend time was spent doing what I love best: rambling around Chicago neighborhoods that I want to know better or leading friends around town on historical tours. I created a personal website designed for guiding people around if I was out of town for one reason or another. It's still there, at:http://gryjhnsn.tripod.com/chicago-history.com. When the job of President of the Chicago History Museum opened up, even though I could not offer museum management experience in my resume, this website became Exhibit A – proof of my passion for Chicago, its neighborhoods and its history.

I was flattered when three of our volunteers – Greg Borzo, Suzanne Haynes and Bernard Turner – asked me to make a contribution to their book, *The Windies' City*. The Windies, of course, is a name that some of our volunteers at the Chicago History Museum give themselves. This book grows out of the same passion that led me to create my little website: what can I do for my friends who, for one reason or another, won't be along during the tours I lead? Sure, there are the official tours they give for the Chicago History Museum, but what about all those rambles that are off the beaten path?

This wonderful book is the answer.

This guidebook will take you to some of the Windies' favorite places to visit in Chicago. One of the Windies will be your guide for each destination. You will get practical information, such as how to find the site and why it is worth visiting. You will hear about the highlights. Because visits like these involve learning something new each time, you will hear some of things that your guide has learned over the years.

No book, of course, is a substitute for a personal tour, but this book was assembled by some of the city's experts in giving historical tours, and you will hear their voices as you read these pages. You will benefit from their experience, as you visit some of their favorite places.

You will visit places you have heard of, but may not have seen, such as Haymarket Square. Graceland is the city's most famous cemetery, but there are others that are full of history, such as Oak Woods. This book will point you to treasures created in Chicago's diverse communities, such as the Bud Billiken Day Parade and the National Museum of Mexican Art. You have probably heard of the Clarke house, which is the oldest building in the city still standing and located in the Prairie Avenue Historic District, but have you heard of the Caldwell Lily Pond? They are all in this book, along with other favorite places to visit.

As you go about Chicago with this book in hand, you will experience the joy of discovering something new in the city. But for some of you, that won't be the end of it! Some of you will want to return and share some of that joy with friends and family. You will want to share something of what you learned from this book, and some new things that you discovered yourself during your first visit. Sharing the experience of your favorite places in this great city will become a passion for you, as it is for the Windies and as it is for me.

When that happens, consider contacting us at the Chicago History Museum. We are always looking for volunteers. We love training new docents. We love designing new tours. We love finding new Windies.

I have officially been invited to become a Windie, and, when time permits, I'll participate in upcoming tours and visits, but in the meantime, I still have a day job here at the museum. In any case, I am flattered that they have asked me to make a contribution.

I know that first-time visitors to Chicago and life-long residents alike will welcome *The Windies' City* and join me in thanking the Windies, not only for this printed guide, but for their service to our Museum and our community.

Alfred Caldwell Lily Pool

Fullerton Avenue
between Stockton Drive
and Lake Shore Drive

Lily Pool and Cascade

Description

The Lily Pool, located just north of Lincoln Park Zoo, is a fine example of Prairie School design. Its features include two pavilions, a cascading waterfall, and a lagoon that wends its way slowly through the multilevel landscaping. There are pathways of Niagara limestone and a council ring, a place for meditation and reflection.

The Victorian garden and lily pond originally built in 1889 in this area had fallen into disrepair. In 1936 – 1938, landscape designer Alfred Caldwell transformed the place into a natural masterpiece, dubbing it a "hidden garden for the megalopolis." In 2002, the Chicago Park District and the Friends of Lincoln Park completed another renovation of the area, which restored it to Caldwell's original design.

Designated a Chicago Landmark in November 2002 and a National Historic Landmark in February 2006, the Lily Pool celebrates the natural beauty of the prairie landscape that was originally shaped by glaciers and the lakefront.

Why I recommend visiting this site

Talk about a hidden treasure, this is one of the most beautiful landscape achievements and scenic sites in Chicago. When you see the beauty of the Lily Pool, you will be immediately captivated. Viewing the before and after

Prairie School Pavillion

photos of the latest renovation convinced me that the Chicago Park District and the Lincoln Park Conservancy did a wonderful job of restoring the area to its original state and preserving a true Chicago landmark. This is

the place to be if you are looking for peace and quiet, broken only by the sounds of trickling water and singing birds. It is also a place for solitude; often, you may be the only person there.

Highlights of the visit

Caldwell was a follower of Jens Jensen, the Prairie School landscape designer, and he incorporated many of Jensen's techniques and design elements into the Lily Pool. Beautiful scenery, native plants and wildlife, meandering waterways, the artistic use of limestone, and the serenity make a visit worthwhile.

Jensen designed many Chicago parks, including his masterpiece, Columbus Park, as well as Humboldt, Garfield, and Douglas parks. He also designed numerous smaller parks in Wisconsin and Iowa and the North Shore estate landscapes of rich and famous Chicagoans such as the Ryersons, the Florsheims, and the Rosenwalds.

Three things I learned

Designed in 1936, and originally named the Zoo Rookery, the area was officially dedicated as the Alfred Caldwell Lily Pool in May 2000.

One of the chief goals of the latest renovation was to provide a resting place for migratory birds that offered the protection of a variety of trees and shrubs, including flowering and fruiting trees, as well as native grasses and flowers in varying heights and sizes, such as those originally chosen by Caldwell. The birds have returned and can truly appreciate their place of respite.

Another Prairie School landscape designed by Caldwell while working for the Chicago Park District is Promontory Point in Hyde Park, which he created from a landfill in 1937. This high point of Burnham Park affords visitors beautiful views of downtown buildings and provides great recreation for bikers, joggers, and picnickers.

Bernard C. Turner

Explore
Bronzeville
King Drive & 35th Street

8th Regiment Armory now Chicago Military Academy

A great place to get a good perspective on Bronzeville is from this intersection, because you can see several of the historic structures that are part of the *Black Metropolis Historic District*, which was granted Chicago Landmark status in September 1998. These include the Victory Monument, the Liberty Life/Supreme Life Insurance Building, and the Sunset Café/Grand Terrace Café.

Description

One question that I am always asked is: "What are the boundaries of Bronzeville?" I answer that the boundaries are approximately the Dan Ryan Expressway on the west, Lake

Michigan on the east, 31st Street on the north, and 51st Street on the south. These are, of course, subject to debate. Another question I am asked is about the origin of the name Bronzeville. Because of its location near the historic home of Senator Stephen A. Douglas, the official name of the neighborhood is Douglas/Grand Boulevard. But because the area was the center of African-American life and culture, the name Bronzeville reflects the institutions and activities of people of color, such as the Miss Bronze America pageants that were held in the past.

Why I recommend visiting this site

Bronzeville is one of the neighborhoods that helps to define Chicago history and

Chicago Bee/Douglas Bank buildings

culture. Located on the Windy City's South Side, this area was the destination for many African Americans who chose to migrate to Chicago from the South during the Great Migration in the early 1900s.

Bronzeville's population

grew from 85,000 in 1900 to 387,000 in 1940. The first home I remember as a child was at Bowen Avenue and Cottage Grove Avenue in that neighborhood.

Highlights of the visit

One of the first things

I discovered when planning this tour was the 14-foot-long bronze map that depicts historical places in Bronzeville. Designed by Greg Lefevre, the map is located in the median at the intersection of 35th Street and King Drive, just across from the Victory Monument. It is part of the Bronzeville Walk of Fame that stretches from 25th Street to 47th Street. The Walk features 91 bronze plaques naming famous residents of the neighborhood. Whenever I have led tours here, the participants could hardly tear themselves away from the map. Everyone recognizes the famous nightclubs such as the Savoy Ballroom and the Club Delisa, entertainment venues such as Chess Records and the Regal Theater, and important groups such as baseball's Negro Leagues and the Chicago Urban League.

Other sites that are part of the *Black Metropolis Historic District* are the Overton Hygienic Building, the Chicago Bee Building/

Douglas National Bank at 36th and State streets, the Wabash Avenue YMCA at 37th Street and Wabash Avenue, the Chicago Defender Building at 34th Street and Wabash Avenue, and the Eighth Regiment Armory at 35th Street and Giles Avenue. These institutions supported, sheltered, and educated African Americans during the Great Migration and throughout the heyday of Bronzeville.

Another enlightening part of the tour was the visit to the Chicago Bee Building, which currently houses a Chicago Public Library branch. We were treated to a history lesson from children's librarian Chris Reynolds, who told the group about the entrepreneurship and productivity of Anthony

Overton, whose cosmetics business and Douglass National Bank were extremely influential in providing jobs and creating wealth in the community.

Map of Bronzeville – 35th and King Drive

We also enjoyed viewing the beautiful collection of quilts in the library's auditorium.

Our next stop was the Wabash Avenue YMCA.

Opened in 1913, it became a center for education and culture in the "Black Metropolis." Carter G. Woodson founded the Association for the Study of Negro Life and Culture there in 1915.

Just before lunch at Pearl's Place on Pershing Road and Michigan Avenue, we visited Wendell Phillips High School. This impressive classic revival structure has history and class! The student body of Phillips has included some of the most famous African Americans in Chicago and in the United States: Nat King Cole; John H. Johnson of Ebony Publishing fame; Dinah Washington; Marla Gibbs of "The Jeffersons" TV show; and Alonso H. Parham, the first African American to attend West Point. The photos preserved on the "Wall of Fame" at Phillips provide a real history lesson about those who graduated from this venerable institution and their contributions to Chicago history.

Three things I learned

While looking at the photos at Wendell Phillips High School, we happened upon some photos of the Savoy Five, who were predecessors of the Harlem Globetrotters. Little did we know that some of the players on Phillips's winning basketball team formed the group that became the world-famous Globetrotters.

We also stopped at the Chicago Military Academy, Bronzeville. The renovated Eighth Regiment Armory is now a Chicago Public High School. It was the first armory in the United States built for an African-American regiment. "The Fighting Eighth", as it came to be known, started as a volunteer militia and, during WWI, became the 370th U.S. Infantry.

Although we did not go inside, we paused outside the South Side Community Arts Center. This Georgian-style revival residence was built in 1892. Dedicated in 1941 with Eleanor Roosevelt present and partially sponsored by the Works Progress Administration (WPA), the Center was a place where artists could develop their talents and display their work. Important artists who worked there include sculptor Richard Hunt, photojournalist Gordon Parks, Archibald Motley, and Margaret Burroughs, founder of the DuSable Museum.

Bernard C. Turner

Wendell Phillips High School

Brown Line 'L'

Brown Line 'L' trains pass through the Clark Junction

Description

The Northwestern Elevated, the precursor to the Brown Line, was built by Charles Tyson Yerkes, a colorful transit baron, who also built the Loop elevated system. It opened in 1900 as the city's fourth 'L' line, ran from downtown to Wilson Avenue, and cost five cents to ride. An extension from Belmont Avenue to Kimball Avenue was added in 1907. Built by private enterprise, without the power of eminent domain, the line zigs and zags through neighborhoods, around churches, over streets, and through alleys.

In its heyday, the 'L' was extremely busy, carrying not only transit but also interurban trains, express service, and freight. It even carried funeral trains loaded with coffins and mourners. To accommodate all this traffic, the line north of the Chicago station is four tracks wide, although some of this trackage has been abandoned.

Today the Brown Line includes 28 stations and 11.3 miles of track. It is the CTA's most successful 'L', accounting for most of its systemwide growth in ridership during the 1990s. There are very few vacant lots along the Brown Line: land is very valuable, thanks, in part, to the proximity of the 'L'.

Why I recommend visiting this site:

The 'L' is perhaps Chicago's greatest, most

The 'L' zigs and zags around buildings, including the Yondorf Block and Hall.

historically significant icon. At more than 114 years of age, it is not just an antique; it is a working antique. Anyone who wants to understand Chicago—with its myriad neighborhoods, rail heritage, and democratic spirit—has to ride and study the 'L'. The Brown Line is the city's most picturesque elevated. There's so much to see, from skyscrapers to vacant lots, the Gold Coast to housing projects, culture to sports, and churches to saloons.

Highlights of the visit

The major objective of the Chicago History Museum's monthly Brown Line tour is to follow the growth of the city north and west. Primarily German, but also Irish, Swedish, Italian and other ethnic groups followed . . . and pushed . . . the city outward. From downtown, up the North Branch of the Chicago River and along former Native American trails such as Lincoln Avenue, these ethnic groups moved northwest, improving their living conditions and pursuing the American Dream.

The forces of housing and transportation fed each other, which is why so many of the streets along the Brown Line, including Kedzie, Fullerton, and Sedgwick, are named for real estate developers. The more 'L' lines were built, the more prairie was subdivided into housing tracts; the more homes, the greater the need for mass transit.

Three things I learned

Many fabulous movies

were shot along the Brown Line. In *Code of Silence*, Chuck Norris dives into the Chicago River from the top of an 'L' car as it passes over the Wells Street Bridge downtown. In *While You Were Sleeping*, Sandra Bullock plays a fetching CTA agent at the Wabash Avenue/Randolph Street station. She falls in love with one of the daily riders and… well, you'll just have to see the movie! In *Just Visiting*, Jean Reno plays a medieval French knight transported by witchcraft to modern-day Chicago. One of the best scenes shows him riding a horse from the Library station onto an 'L' car that had to be specially reinforced to handle the spirited steed.

Even regular riders of the Brown Line can frequently see new things— from the historical to the

Fare register at the renovated Quincy station.

bizarre—if they watch carefully as the buildings, gardens, streets, roofs, and signs of the city pass by. Some stores have display windows aimed at transit riders (harkening back to a day when transit had 90 percent or more of the market), and some buildings are stamped with long-gone street names. A few such unexpected treats to watch for include a stable, a parking garage designed to resemble a car, and a water tower painted with images of pencils on top of an old pencil factory.

The 'L' was elevated to avoid street congestion and

for safety. By 1893 Chicago had more than 1,500 railroad crossings at grade level. Hundreds of people, mostly kids, were killed or maimed crossing or playing on the tracks. An 1893 law required Chicago's railroads to be elevated—not only the mass transit lines being constructed but also existing freight railroads. An example of this elevation can be seen on the old Chicago & Northwestern line that parallels the Brown Line from Roscoe Street to Sunnyside Avenue. Factories moved to the industrial corridor to take advantage of the freight service. Some of these factories continue to operate, although an increasing number have been converted to condominiums.

Greg Borzo

Bud Billiken Day Parade

Channel 7 float

Location

The Bud Billiken Day Parade takes place on the second Saturday of August every year. The parade begins at Oakwood Boulevard and King Drive.

Description

The *Chicago Defender*, founded in 1905 by Robert S. Abbott, sought out and reported news of the African-American community and national news of interest to Blacks that was not reported in other local papers. In 1923, Abbott started the Bud Billiken Club for the young people who sold his newspaper. The club became so popular that Abbott decided to start an annual parade and picnic. The first Bud Billiken Day Parade took place in 1929. It featured the actors who played the main characters on the "Amos and Andy" TV show as honored guests. Since 1945, the parade has been sponsored by the Chicago Defender Charities organization. It is now the largest parade in the United States, with more than 160 floats and vehicles and street-side viewers numbering as many as 1.5 million.

The original parade route, from 31st Street and Michigan Avenue to Washington Park, was changed to its present route in the 1930s. Many famous Chicago and national figures have been featured in the parades over the years, including boxing greats Joe Louis and Muhammad Ali;

big band leader Duke Ellington and R&B singers such as Brandy; local organizations such as the Shriners and University of Chicago Hospitals; and politicians galore. I remember going to the 2004 parade during the U.S. Senate campaign between Barack Obama and Alan Keyes. Well, you can just imagine the contrast in the reception that the two experienced.

Why I recommend visiting this site

Every kid loves a parade, and this one is practically the granddaddy of them all, at least by Chicago standards. 2005 marked the parade's 76th anniversary. The Bud Billiken Day Parade is a Chicago tradition, a great day of celebration, and, for children, the time

Jesse White Tumblers fly and flip along King Drive

to get ready for the beginning of a new school year. The sights, sounds, and smells; the dazzling costumes; and the precision of the marching bands of today's parades bring back fond memories of my childhood. The people along the parade route are very

friendly, and the spirit of the day is electric. The parade is also a picnic. You can literally taste your way along the route, sampling all kinds of snack foods, as well as grilled specialties such as hot links, rib tips, and jerk chicken.

Highlights of the visit

There are many flashy marchers, dynamic bands and extravagantly decorated floats in the parade, but the highlight of the 2004 parade for me was seeing performers from the Universoul Circus, a professional traveling circus company that features unique African and African-American performers. There were trapeze artists, African dancers, and clowns on stilts lined up right behind us.

Always a thrilling act, the internationally known Jesse White Tumblers flipped, bounced, and tumbled from the start along King Drive to the finish in Washington Park. The tumbling team was founded in 1959 by Illinois Secretary of State Jesse White to help troubled youth better their lives and stay focused on the future. Over the years, more than 8,600 young people from tough neighborhoods, such as the "projects" (Cabrini Green and the Henry Horner Homes), have benefited from the discipline and rigor of training and high academic expectations. The Jesse White Tumblers have appeared at major professional sporting events, college football games, and even on "Late Night with David Letterman."

The politicians definitely make a statement as well. Whether they are running for office, jockeying for new positions, or simply supporting the community, politicians show up in force. Governor Blagojevich walked the parade route waving and wielding his influence. The contenders were there in classic and

Float with oldest living Bud Billiken, Dave Kellum

vintage cars to be seen and remembered; Senator Barack Obama and his wife were crowd pleasers to be sure. People line up as many as eight to ten back from the curb to shout and wave at the politicians and at celebrities from TV and radio.

Three things I learned

The name Bud Billiken was thought up by Robert S. Abbott and his managing editor, Lucius Harper. They took the name from a pointy-headed Chinese character or doll that was originally called Joss—the "god of things as they ought to be" and "patron saint" to children. Billiken materials were originally manufactured by the Billiken Company of Chicago, which produced stuffed dolls and other objects, including salt and pepper shakers. The design for the character was the 1908 brainchild of Florence Pretz, a Kansas City illustrator and art teacher.

The St. Louis University sports teams are named the Billikens. The name originated in about 1910 with two local sportswriters who dubbed the football team Bender's Billikens because they thought coach John Bender, with his broad grin and squinty eyes, resembled the Billiken character.

The Billiken character continues to be popular in Japan, where it is believed to bring luck and good fortune.

Bernard C. Turner

Charnley-Persky
1365 North Astor Street

Despite its impressive size, the Charnley-Persky House Museum has only 11 rooms.

Description

In 1890 James Charnley bought a lot at Astor and Schiller streets for $27,500. The area was being built up with the freestanding homes and rowhouses of wealthy people, most of them designed in Victorian or traditional styles with ornate features and abundant decorations. Foremost among these homes were the ostentatious Potter Palmer mansion, built a block east on Lake Shore Drive in 1882–1886, and the Cardinal's mansion at 1555 North State Parkway, built in 1882–1885. (The Palmer mansion was demolished in 1950; but the Cardinal's residence is still standing.)

Charnley grew up in an octagonal house in New Haven, Connecticut, and wanted something different from these mammoth, showy residences. He must have appreciated modern architecture because he hired Adler & Sullivan to design a house for his family. By this point in his career, Louis Sullivan rarely designed homes, but since he and the Charnleys were good friends, he agreed to do so in this case.

Charnley and Sullivan apparently wanted to establish a strong visual presence in what was becoming one of the city's most prestigious neighborhoods. They did not, however, want to make a statement about wealth or social status, as Charnley's social and business peers were doing in this ultra-exclusive residential area. Instead, their house was to be relatively small and plain.

From 1891 to 1892 Sullivan, the master, and Frank Lloyd Wright, one of his employees, worked on the house together. It is very difficult, in fact, to tell which great architect is responsible for various features of the house, much less for its overall design. The ovals and oak leaf patterns would have been Sullivan's touch, while the horizontal lines and geometric shapes would have been Wright's doing. But the scant archival record of the house's history and architectural background leaves this and other questions open for interpretation. In any event, Wright claimed he designed the house—but he did not do so until after Sullivan

Generous use of wood and a central light-well define the interior of this innovative house.

died.

Why I recommend visiting this site

After visiting the Frank Lloyd Wright houses in Oak Park, Illinois, several times, usually with out-of-town visitors in tow, I was surprised to learn that there was an important house with a Wright connection on the North Side of Chicago. Since the Charnley-Persky House is close to the Chicago History Museum, the Windies' home base, I decided to learn more about it.

The first time I went looking for the house I walked right by without noticing it. Then, I was disappointed to find that I couldn't go in because of restricted visiting hours. That's when I decided to make visiting the house a Windies activity; as a group, we would be able to schedule our own tour and, afterwards, discuss this easily overlooked gem among ourselves.

Highlights of the visit

It's no wonder that Wright wanted to take credit for the Charnley house. It is innovative yet beautiful, audacious but refined. The exterior is plain brick and limestone, and although it lacks much ornamentation, appears elegant. A balcony over the entrance captures your attention, but not in an overbearing way. Simplicity and symmetry reign.

The moment we walked into the house we were greeted by a very unusual interior, dominated by a soaring light-well that extends through all three floors. The light in this vertical atrium illuminates an abundance of broad, richly toned wooden railings, borders, edges, and moldings. We learned that this extensive use of wood was due to the fact that James Charnley made his fortune in the lumber industry.

A fireplace greets you as you enter. Rather than featuring a grand staircase with a traditional banister, the house hides the stairways to its second and third floors by a wall and a screen of spindles, respectively. Abundant natural light contrasts with darker, channeled spaces. The close quarters make it clear that the house offered comfortable living and working quarters rather than large spaces for entertaining.

As with any good tour, we left with more questions than we had when we arrived. For example, on exiting the house we saw that the east wall had been left bare in anticipation of the construction of a neighboring building. This never happened, leaving an unattractive brick wall with only one window (which was added later). What would the architects have done differently if they had designed this as a freestanding building? Did Charnley and his architects want to annoy their more traditional neighbors with a modern plan, or did they simply design the house for their own appreciation?

Three things I learned

According to Wright, the Charnley house is "the first modern house in America." From the beginning, it has been recognized as exceptional, even revolutionary, by experts and amateurs alike.

In 1995, the Society of Architectural Historians purchased the house, which had been beautifully restored in 1988 by Skidmore, Owings & Merrill. Seymour H. Persky provided the funds for the purchase, on the conditions that the house be open to the public and that the society move its headquarters from Philadelphia to Chicago.

This was the second Charnley house in Chicago. The first, at 1200 North Lake Shore Drive, a large traditional affair with wraparound porches and a suburban or resort-like look to it, was designed in 1882 to 1883 by Burnham & Root. It was just three blocks south of Palmer's mansion, which was built at the same time. That made Charnley one of the urban pioneers who, together with Potter and Bertha Palmer, helped draw Chicago's elite away from the city's first Gold Coast—on Prairie Avenue—to the area surrounding Astor and Schiller streets that is now known as the Gold Coast.

Greg Borzo

Chicago Cultural Center

Michigan Avenue between Randolph and Washington streets

Chicago Cultural Center view from Millenium Park

Description

In the late 1800s, the decision by the city of Chicago and the state of Illinois to put a library and a Civil War memorial in the same building presented a design challenge: How could one building serve both purposes equally and still express the unique personality of each? The answer was to create what were actually two buildings under one roof. Each wing had its own facade, dome, and staircase, as well as its own decorations. Roman architecture influenced the south side (Washington Street) exterior and Greek architecture influenced the north side (Randolph Street).

The building, which was designed by the Boston firm of Shepley, Rutan & Coolidge, was completed in 1897. The south side became the first permanent home of the Chicago Public Library: the north side was originally dedicated as a memorial for the Grand Army of the Republic (GAR).

Today, the building, which houses the main office of the Chicago Department of Cultural Affairs, is the nation's first free municipal cultural center. The Cultural Center is listed on the National Register of Historic Places and is a Chicago Landmark. It offers several hundred programs every year including classical, jazz, and contemporary music performances; art exhibitions; dance; theatre; films; lectures; family and holiday programs; and special events—all free.

Why I recommend visiting this site

The Cultural Center is a lively place, with a busy schedule of talks, musical performances, and art exhibits. Even if you attend a lot of the center's programs, you may not realize all there is to this historically important and architecturally significant building. A tour makes you aware of the multiple uses, the world-classic mosaics, and the many ornate rooms, as well as of the fact that the two wings of the building were built for separate purposes.

How lucky we are to have this palace. Stop in on any day to enjoy music, art, or theater in this beautiful space. Free, guided tours are given on Wednesdays,

View from Randolph Street

Fridays, and Saturdays, and self-guided audio tours and brochures are always available.

Highlights of the visit

Preston Bradley Hall, named for a prominent Chicago theologian, is spectacularly adorned with a 38-foot Tiffany stained glass dome with cut glass set at slight angles to reflect light. The walls are white Carrara marble inlaid with mosaics of colored stone. The large, graceful arches that set off the room bear the names of

23

Tiffany glass dome

great writers of the Western world. My favorite detail is the inscriptions in 10 languages that extol the wisdom found in books. This inscription, for example, is from the Greek biographer, Plutarch: "The advice which their friends have not the courage to give to kings is found written in books."

The building's designers wanted a place so beautiful that it would be a work of art in itself. Although grand enough for royalty, it has always been used for free municipal purposes and was once referred to as The People's Palace. As big as it is, you can go from one magnificent room to another, finding something equally impressive in each. The Sidney R. Yates Gallery, for instance, is a replica of an assembly hall in the 14th-century Doge's Palace in Venice.

The book, *The People's Palace*, available in the gift shop, is full of great pictures and historical details.

Three things I learned

There is a unique dome and staircase for each side of the building, fitting the personality and purpose of its original use. The GAR rotunda and hall are among the building's most magnificent attractions. This space was originally the meeting and reception space for the GAR organization, as well as a museum of Civil War artifacts. Many of these artifacts can now be found at the new Harold Washington Library on State Street. The glass tile blocks in the GAR rotunda floor were originally designed to allow light to pass through to the floor below. Now, the domes in both rotundas are covered to protect them from possible damage.

The site of the building is on, arguably, some of the most valuable and attractive property in Chicago. It was available in the late 19th century because it was part of the Fort Dearborn property. After Fort Dearborn was dismantled, the property was given to the city and, for a while, was used as a park. For a period of time, Dearborn Park was not only the first park in the city but the only one. That is why the land was eventually used for a public building; it could not be sold for commercial use.

The Grand Staircase leading from the Washington Street lobby to Preston Bradley Hall was built by foreign artisans, many of whom are the ancestors of current Chicago residents. The multicolored mosaics are made of Favrile glass, colored stone, and mother of pearl. The green medallions in the staircase are of rare emerald marble from Connemara, Ireland. You can pause at each landing to enjoy the mosaics displayed on the underside of the open staircase above.

Suzanne Haynes

Chicago Temple
77 West Washington in the Chicago Temple Building

Chicago Temple spire in the sky.

Description

In 1831, a dozen Methodists who lived near Fort Dearborn responded to two circuit riders to organize a "class" that met in the living room of one of its members. The group grew quickly, and in 1834 built a log cabin at the intersection of what are now Clark and North Water streets. In 1838, they floated the cabin across the river and rolled it onto the corner of Clark and Washington streets.

This has been the Methodist Corner ever since.

By 1845, the community had grown large enough to build a more conventional structure. In 1858, they committed to staying anchored on this corner, in a rapidly growing and changing city, by building a four-story, multi-use structure with stores and businesses on the lower floors and church space on the upper floors. This building was destroyed in the fire of 1871. The 1858 plan was used to build the current structure, the fourth on the site.

Why I recommend visiting this site

If you happen to be at the corner of Washington and Clark streets, and if you look up, you will see a church spire that reaches 568 feet above street level on the top of a skyscraper. Who wouldn't be curious enough to find out the story of this congregation? Not being a very old city, or a European city, Chicago does not have a lot of ancient

View from Clark Street

churches in its business districts. This church is Chicago's oldest established congregation and has been located in the same place since the city was incorporated in 1837.

A 92-year-old docent took our group around the church. She shared a lot of personal recollections of the church and some of her religious views, making for an amusing and interesting tour. Depending on the docent, this tour might provide more information about the founding and principles of the modern Methodist Church than historical or architectural information, but I suppose that a lot of visitors take the tour for spiritual reasons. Tours are at 2:00 P.M. daily.

Highlights of the visit

The Sky Chapel, which was a gift from the Walgreen family, is the highest place of worship above ground level in the world. You can make the pilgrimage via two elevators and a set of stairs to the octagonal chapel located under the spire, 400 feet above the streets of the city. It was much smaller than I expected, however, and if, for example, you wanted to get married there, your guest list would have to be limited to about 30 people.

There are 16 stained glass windows, with themes representing the beginning of Christianity from its Hebrew traditions through to this church's development in the "New World" city of Chicago. You never escape the strong sense of mission the church has for its community.

There is a companion altarpiece in the Sky Chapel to the one in the main floor sanctuary. In the main sanctuary, Christ is looking over Jerusalem and weeping for humanity and its inability to find peace. In the Sky Chapel altarpiece, Christ is weeping for the same reason, but the city he is overlooking is a Chicago view from the northeast windows of the chapel.

Three things I learned

The current structure, built by the renowned architectural firm Holabird & Roche, mixes French Gothic with the practicality of an American skyscraper. When it was dedicated in 1924, the Temple was the tallest building in Chicago. The first four floors are used for church work; floors 5–21 are offices, mainly used by lawyers, since the church is surrounded by city, county, and state government buildings. Clarence Darrow occupied an office on the 6th floor. The senior pastor and his family live in an apartment on the 23rd–25th floors. These floors are in the spire, where the floor space is not as big, resulting in the family's living in somewhat of a townhouse-like structure.

The first floor sanctuary is open seven days a week, 14 hours a day, and serves as a true sanctuary for the people of Chicago. Many street people seeking a place to sit and get warm were gathered the afternoon I was there, as well as others coming in to pray and meditate. It is spectacularly decorated for a Protestant church, in an Arts and Crafts style, with beautiful stained glass windows designed by the Giannini and Hilgart Studios of Chicago. The focal point in the sanctuary is the altar carving by German artist Alois Lang referred to above. It depicts text from the Gospel of Luke when Christ descends from the Mount of Olives and calls for the understanding that makes for peace.

Institutions this parish helped found include the Garrett Evangelical Theological Seminary, Wesley Hospital, Northwestern University and the Methodist Home for Children.

Suzanne Haynes

Explore

Chinese-American Museum of Chicago

238 West 23rd Street, Chicago

Chinese garment in Chinese-American Museum

Description

The Chinese-American Museum opened in May 2005, making it less than a year old when we visited. It is off Wentworth Avenue, the main shopping street, in a small storefront building that used to be a supermarket. There have already been some impressive exhibits here: the first, "Paper Sons," about the Chinese in the Midwest, consisted of objects assembled from a dozen public and private collections. When we were there only the first floor of the museum was open; work was ongoing on the upper floors. The two exhibits featured were the impressive "Silk and Wood" and

"Tofu." The tofu exhibit actually made me want to go out and eat some—which I did. (Incidentally, you can still get handmade tofu in Chicago.)

Why I recommend visiting this site

This site is located in yet another great neighborhood filled with wonderful, exotic shops. Besides the visual architecture, you know you are in Chinatown because almost everyone on the street is speaking Chinese. This makes it distinctive from many of the other diverse ethnic neighborhoods in the city and immediately puts you in the mood for learning about the Chinese immigrant experience.

Because the museum is only open from Friday to

Moy Association Building

Sunday, with varying hours, it is best to check out their Web site before your visit.

Highlights of the Visit

When we visited, the two staff members we met were people who were

largely responsible for establishing the museum and planning its exhibits. Both have made impressive contributions to explaining the culture and history of the Chinese in Chicago. One is the museum's president,

Chuimei Ho, one of several authors of *Chinese in Chicago*, a booklet that is part of the popular "Images of America" series. The other is Ben Bronson, a curator of Asian Archaeology and Ethnology at the Field Museum.

Because the museum is new and small, we had the opportunity to receive the attention and knowledge of these experts.

Part of our tour consisted of walking around the neighborhood, especially along Wentworth Avenue, noting the many old and architecturally interesting buildings. We stopped in a specialty teashop, and we checked out other intriguing places with wares you won't find in other parts of town. We ended up in Chinatown Square Plaza, where we had a choice of several ethnic restaurants for lunch, and then some of us visited the lovely new Ping Tom Memorial Park, along the south branch of the Chicago River.

Wentworth Avenue is filled with interesting architecture with Chinese

Wentworth Street looking north

motifs. Most of these buildings were built in the late 1920s. Three of the more interesting are the Moy Association Building, with its impressive third-floor balcony and Chinese-style tiles in green, yellow, and white; the Won Kow Restaurant; and the Pui Tak Building. The Won Kow Restaurant, which opened in 1928, is the second oldest continuously operated Chinese restaurant in Chicago; it has second- and third-floor balconies and a tile roof supported by Chinese brackets. The Pui Tak Center, the only building designated as a landmark, once housed the powerful On Leong Merchants Association. It was seized in 1992 by the federal government during a questionable, but widely publicized, prosecution for gambling.

Three things I learned

Whether you first see it by car or from the Red Line 'L' stop, the Chinatown Gateway, built across Wentworth Avenue and Cermak Road, is an obvious clue that you have arrived in Chinatown. The four characters that appear on the gateway read *Tian-xia-wei-gong*. This phrase from Sun Yat-sen, the first president of the Chinese Republic, translates to "for the people."

Chinese immigrants first started arriving in the Chicago area around the 1870s and, before moving south to this area, lived in the Loop and worked in laundries. Today, there are no longer any Chinese laundries in Chicago; many of the Chinese people make their living in the food industry.

At one time, Al Capone's headquarters was in the Lexington Hotel, a few blocks east of Chinatown, at Cermak Road and Michigan Avenue. Cermak was one of the few east–west streets to cross many of the north–south railroad tracks in this part of the city. Capone's gang would often have traveled it, especially when attending church or going out for Chinese food. The Madonna Incoronata Church at Wentworth Avenue and Alexander Street—now St. Therese Church—was the Italian-speaking Catholic church closest to Capone's headquarters. The crucifix behind the altar at St. Therese's was donated by Mrs. Thersen Capone, Al's mother.

Suzanne Haynes

Civic Opera House
20 North Wacker Drive

Ardis Krainik Theatre

Description

The Civic Opera House, home of Chicago's Lyric Opera, takes up the entire block between Washington and Madison streets. The limestone skyscraper includes a 45-story office building and two 22-story wings. The west side of the Opera House, which is shaped like a throne, faces the south branch of the Chicago River. The building, which opened in November 1929, just six days after the stock market crash, was the vision of Samuel Insull, its billionaire builder. There was a major substation of the Commonwealth Edison Company, the power utility started by Insull, in the basement.

Fire Curtain

2nd balcony as they are in front of the orchestra. Insull's democratic mandate did assure his five other requisites: safety, excellent sight lines, comfortable seating, gracious surroundings.

A close viewing of both the exterior and interior ornamentation reveals objects such as lyres, trumpets, laurel wreaths, and other decorative features characteristic of the Art Nouveau and Art Deco styles. Upon first entering the Daniel F. and Ada L. Rice Grand Foyer of the opera house, you will no doubt be impressed by the 40-foot travertine columns, Austrian crystal chandeliers, and the grand double staircase. You will certainly feel that you are in for an elegant evening.

Insull wanted the building to be "democratic in scope." His plan was for the commercial office tower to financially support the opera hall. Having sat in a variety of the more than 3,500 seats, I can say that the prices and views today are certainly not "democratic," but the acoustics are as good in the

Why I recommend visiting this site

I love opera and thought it would be a coup to arrange something special for the Chicago History Museum volunteers. There is much to learn about the Opera House's architecture and design and its colorful builder. It is also interesting to experience the backstage tour of the Lyric Opera and to discover what goes into making an opera production.

Another way to see the opera house is to buy a ticket. It is possible to buy inexpensive seats and to walk around the auditorium before listening to renowned music in a world-class house.

Highlights of the visit

Backstage at the Lyric! The auditorium takes up a third of the Lyric Opera space. We were able to go onto the stage and also saw the view from the cat walk six stories above the stage. It was amazing to look at the rigging for the scenery and to learn how it is moved around. We saw the dressing rooms for the chorus and supernumeraries and the wardrobe rooms, and we realized how much work goes into every production, by everyone from wig masters to seamstresses. We toured the stars' dressing rooms, heard stories about various singers' quirks, and saw demonstrations of many of the numerous props.

Three things I learned

Jules Guerin was the artist who painted the famous fire curtain mural depicting the triumphal

A night at the opera

35

procession scene from Verdi's opera Aida, which was the first opera performed in the Civic Opera House. Guerin was also responsible for the entire color scheme of the opera house, which is largely salmon, vermilion, orange, and gold. It is interesting that, although color is something we may not notice initially, it somehow creeps into our consciousness and affects how we feel about a given space. This is very important in a theater, as staging is so much a part of the whole experience.

The box seats at the Lyric are much farther from the stage than those in most opera houses. Insull felt that the goings-on in box seats tended to distract the audience from the music. Those were the days! Now one must sit as still as possible and not make any noise.

It was interesting to hear about the colorful personality of Samuel Insull, known as the Prince of Electricity. Insull, who was born in England, idolized Thomas Edison and came to America in 1881, at age 22, to be Edison's personal secretary. By 1889, he had a reputation as a business dynamo. In 1892, he was sent to Chicago to become president of the struggling Chicago Edison Company. He became a very important Chicago figure, involved in utilities, transportation, and civic issues, but he failed to keep his personal fortune separate from his corporate accounts and, a few years after the crash, he was in ruins. He left for Europe but was indicted on charges of embezzlement and began an 18-month flight to avoid extradition. After an amazing chase, he was finally brought back in 1934 to stand trial and was acquitted of all charges. He died in Paris in 1938. Ironically, he was virtually penniless and forgotten.

Allegedly, Insull claimed that upon his death his spirit would sit in the building's "throne," where he would watch over the growth of the city. If you take one of the three Lyric tours available to the public each year, you will learn Insull's full story. To arrange a tour, visit the Lyric's Web site or call the box office.

Suzanne Haynes

Explore
Clarke House
Museum
1827 S. Indiana Avenue

The Clarke House has survived two fires and two moves.

Description

In 1836, Henry B. Clarke, a wealthy hardware dealer, and his wife, Caroline, came to Chicago from New York and built their house on 20 acres of prairie at 16th Street and Michigan Avenue. Shortly after moving into their new home, but before the dwelling was completed, Mr. Clarke went bankrupt in the economic panic of 1837. The Clarkes managed to keep their home, however, in part by selling land around it.

After Henry Clarke's death in 1849, Mrs. Clarke continued to work on the house, but only on a limited basis, as funds became available. As a result, the Clarkes' plans for the structure were not fully realized until a long time after they moved in. That is why the house has been restored to its completed 1850–1860 state rather than to its earlier, unfinished form.

The house, which has survived two fires, is Chicago's only Greek Revival building. Typical of this type of architecture, the house is made of sandstone, and it is symmetrical, orderly, and pleasing to the eye. The interior has high ceilings, deeply carved woodwork, built-in sliding doors, and floor-to-ceiling windows.

Despite its historical

The dining room has large windows because artificial light was so expensive.

and architectural importance, Clarke House is often overlooked and is visited infrequently. One reason for this is that it was not designed by a famous architect. In fact, no one knows who designed the house. In addition, the small, plain home is over-shadowed by the nearby mansions of the Prairie Avenue Historic District, which was once Chicago's Gold Coast and home to the likes of Potter Palmer and Marshall Field.

It was—and still is—hard to compete with the Romanesque Glessner House and the chateau-like Kimball residence, both of which still stand nearby on Prairie Avenue. Nevertheless, Clarke House, with its columns, gables and cupola, displays an elegance and grace all its own. While the massive Glessner House was designed for privacy and security, and the Kimball Mansion was designed to impress the neighbors, the relatively simple Clarke House was probably designed, in part, to help tame the prairie and civilize the rowdy frontier town of Chicago.

Tours of the Clarke House focus on its architecture, construction, and furnishings, as well as on the social history of Chicago before the Civil War. They also cover the personal story of the Clarkes and their children. Tours begin at the Glessner House Museum at 1800 S. Prairie Avenue.

Why I recommend visiting this site

Jean Baptiste Point DuSable's homestead is long

gone. So are Wolf Tavern—and both Forts Dearborn. Although such legendary structures from Chicago's earliest days have disappeared, there is one building still standing that is nearly as old.

The Clarke House was built in 1836, one year before Chicago was incorporated as a city. That makes it the city's oldest building and, therefore, the perfect place for a bunch of Chicago history buffs to begin a collective exploration of "their kinda town." Accordingly, the Windies began their monthly outings here in the summer of 2001.

Highlight of the visit

The Clarke House is so rich in history and architecture that it is difficult to pick a single highlight. Nevertheless, one of the most interesting things about this remarkable building is the fact that it has been moved twice.

When the Clarke House was built at 16th Street and Michigan Avenue, the unsettled area was considered "out in the country." By 1872, what was then the world's fastest-growing city had engulfed the area, so new owners moved the house to 45th Street and South Wabash Avenue. Then, in 1977, the house was moved again to its present location, not far from its original site.

To accomplish the most recent relocation, movers had to hoist the house over what are now the Green Line 'L' tracks, which had been constructed in 1892–3, after the first move. On December 4, 1977, the second move commenced. The house was raised on jacks and pulled across the 'L' tracks. Unfortunately, the low temperature caused the hydraulic equipment on the other side of the tracks to freeze, so the house could not be lowered until two weeks later, when the weather warmed up! A display area in the gallery on the lower level of the house provides a description and photographs of this remarkable feat.

Incidentally, the fact that the house was moved twice highlights the fact that Chicago once had a thriving industry dedicated to

This parlor shows furnishings from the late 1830s.

moving houses and buildings—expertise that came in handy when the city was raised in the 1850s, 60s, and 70s.

Three things I learned

In 1999, the City of Chicago dedicated the extensive grounds surrounding the Clarke House as the Hillary Rodham Clinton Park and Gardens. Clinton, who is from Park Ridge, Illinois, was then the First Lady and had donated some flowers for the grounds. Oops! It turns out that the city has a policy against naming a park after a living person. So in 2001 the beautiful, four-acre grounds were renamed the Chicago Women's Park and Gardens.

In addition to serving originally as a residence and now as a museum, the Clarke House has been a parsonage, parish hall, and community center. Built to last, it has survived two moves and two fires and has been renovated several times. Currently, it is in magnificent shape. Today, the City of Chicago owns the house and grounds, and the Department of Cultural Affairs operates it. The house is a Chicago Landmark and is listed on the National Register of Historic Places.

Displays in the gallery carry you back to Chicago's origins and portray the life of an upper-middle class family, such as the Clarkes, in the 1850s and 60s. There you will also find an informative timeline that intertwines the histories of the house and the city.

Greg Borzo

Dawes House

225 Greenwood Street, Evanston

Dawes House

Description

The Charles Gates Dawes House, a three-and-a-half story home on a two-acre lakefront site, is quite impressive. It is also eye-catching, because it is constructed of brightly colored orange brick. The house, designed in the style of a French chateau by Henry Edwards-Ficken, an architect from New York, was built in 1896. It has 25 rooms, including six bedrooms and seven bathrooms, and it has 11 fireplaces. Most of the first floor is paneled in oak and contains the great hall, the east parlor (which looks out on Lake Michigan), the west parlor, library, dining room, kitchen, day room, half bath, and butler's pantry. The family living quarters are on the second floor, while the third floor has what were servants' quarters, a ballroom, and a billiards room.

Why I recommend visiting this site

If you have never taken a leisurely drive through the eastern part of Evanston along Sheridan Road, you really have not experienced everything that living in or visiting Chicago has to offer. Homes in the area range from quaint to charming to fabulously beautiful. The Dawes House ranks with the fabulously beautiful. It's also a national historic landmark. As an extra bonus, there's the lakefront and a park of the same name as the house to be enjoyed while visiting the area.

View from Dawes Park in Evanston

Highlights of the visit

The most interesting part of the tour was learning about the life of Charles Dawes and his contributions to Chicago history, U.S. politics, and world affairs. One might say that Dawes's greatest achievement was being elected Calvin Coolidge's vice president in 1924. But there was much more to the man than that. He served in an engineering regiment in WWI and later wrote the Dawes Plan, a plan for the economic development of Europe, for which he won the Nobel Peace Prize in 1926. Dawes was also a composer and an author, a true Renaissance man. His most famous work is the song, "It's All in the

Great Hall with spectacular staircase

Game," which has been performed by great musicians of many different generations, including Nat King Cole and Elton John. Dawes and his wife were also active in charities that benefited the unfortunate and the unemployed.

Dawes was very involved in Chicago business. He founded what was to become Continental Bank, and he and his oil tycoon brother, Rufus, worked with the exposition board of the Century of Progress World's Fair of 1933 as financial committee chairmen. Due to the Dawes's prestige and managerial prowess, and to the use they made of their wealth, the fair was a success, in spite of the economic climate of a country gripped by the Great Depression.

Three things I learned

The Dawes House is now the home of the Evanston Historical Society, which was founded in 1898 and maintains a vast collection of documents and artifacts that tell the story of Evanston from its early days as a stagecoach stop, to its incorporation in 1863, to the present day.

Dawes purchased the 19,000-square-foot mansion, the largest residential home in Evanston, in 1909, for the mere sum of $75,000. The original owner was Reverend Robert Sheppard, treasurer of Northwestern University. Northwestern has helped to maintain the building and holds occasional receptions there.

When other charges would not stick, it was Dawes who suggested that gangster Al Capone be prosecuted for tax evasion. Besides serving as vice president, Dawes was the first director of the Bureau of the Budget (now the Office of Management and Budget) and U.S. ambassador to Great Britain from 1929 to 1931.

Bernard C. Turner

Explore
Downtown
River Walk

**Wolf Point, where the Chicago River splits into the north and south
branches**

Description

The tour started, appropriately enough, at Michigan Avenue, on the north side of the river. After all, that is where Jean Baptiste Point DuSable, Chicago's first non-native permanent settler, lived from 1782 to 1800. A French-speaking black man, Point DuSable was highly regarded for his trapping and trading skills. By the time he sold his settlement and moved to St. Charles, Missouri, Point DuSable had amassed considerable holdings.

As we walked west along the riverbank, we learned that, years ago, architects had the habit of turning their backs to the river. Small wonder; the river was dirty, smelly, and unsightly. Buildings faced the cross streets, and their architects left flat, unadorned facades along the river, with no public access to the waterway. Today, designers are required to beautify the riverside of their buildings, include a public passage, and enhance the splendor of the river.

Why I recommend visiting this site

Chicagoans frequently visit, shop in, and drive through the downtown area, but they typically do not appreciate the rich history that is on display literally everywhere you turn. You can better understand the architecture, politics, commerce, literature, geography and, of course, history of Chicago by touring the main branch of the Chicago River.

Note that tour routes vary, depending on which tour you take; the Chicago Architecture Foundation and Friends of the River, among others, offer tours.

Highlights of the visit

One highlight was realizing how built up the downtown is. Chicago's original settlers lived, traveled, and traded at river level. Today, the streets and sidewalks of State Street, Michigan Avenue, and Upper Wacker Drive are up to 20 or 30 feet above river level. The main reason for building at these levels was to get above the mud and occasional flooding.

Bridges dominate the downtown section of the river. The most common type of bridge was originally the swing bridge, which pivoted from a landing in the middle of the river. As boats became larger, however, these manmade

A plaque at LaSalle Street and Wacker Drive marks the site of the Eastland Disaster.

islands blocked the way for river traffic. In 1863, one such bridge over Rush Street collapsed from the weight of a herd of cattle that rushed onto the deck. Clearly, a better design was needed.

Starting in the 1900s, the trunnion bascule bridge became Chicago's most popular bridge style. This design allows the two spans to open upwards by pivoting on axles (trunnions) using a counterweight buried in the riverbank to lift the deck span. The system is so efficient that it only takes a tiny motor to open and close the bridge.

The most attractive trunnion bascule bridge, which was based on the Alexander III Bridge in Paris, spans the river at Michigan Avenue. From there going west, the bridges become less ornate and more industrial looking. The Michigan Avenue Bridge, for example, conceals its iron support structure below deck, while the iron trusses of the LaSalle Street Bridge are in full view above the deck.

It was exciting to actually walk out to Wolf Point, the social and commercial focus of early Chicago in the 1830s, when four taverns graced the river junction. Later, railroads and warehouses populated the area. Although Wolf Point is dominated by a parking lot today, a path along the river makes the historical site accessible to the public.

Just north of Wolf Point, we stopped along the river at Kinzie Street, where the flooding of Chicago's underground tunnels erupted in 1992, causing an estimated $800 million in damages.

But Chicago's worst maritime disaster occurred on the south side of the river at LaSalle Street. In 1915, the steamship *Eastland* capsized while loading Western Electric employees headed for a company excursion to Michigan City, Indiana. A staggering 844 people died, trapped underwater or knocked about as the ship keeled into the water. A plaque that memorializes the largely forgotten victims was only recently installed along the sidewalk at LaSalle Street and Wacker Drive.

Our tour ended back on Michigan Avenue (across the river from where it had begun) at the site of Fort Dearborn. In 1803, U.S. troops constructed a wooden fort here that was the young government's westernmost military outpost. The fort attracted military personnel as well as businesses to supply them. As a result, Chicago quickly became a center of activity, attracting traders, settlers, and speculators. Bronze markers embedded in the sidewalk show the outlines of the fort, where this activity began more than 200 years ago.

Three things I learned

At one time, the river was so full of traffic that you could cross from one bank to the other by stepping from boat to boat. In fact, in 1871, more ships arrived at Chicago than at New York, San Francisco, Baltimore, Charleston, and Mobile *combined*.

Chicago may be the greatest city ever founded along a short river. The main branch of the river is only one and one-half miles long. The headwaters of the South Branch are at about 32nd Street and Kedzie Avenue; those of the North Branch are in Waukegan.

To save money, the city uses a team of roving bridge tenders who rush from one control tower to the next, opening bridges for boats as they move along the river. Although many restrictions apply, boats have a special status; they must be allowed to pass, no matter how small they are or how many cars will be delayed when a bridge opens.

Greg Borzo

DuSable Museum of African-American History

740 East 56th Street,
in Washington Park

DuSable Museum Entrance

Description

DuSable Museum is located just a few blocks from the site of the great Midway, designed by Daniel Burnham for the World's Columbian Exposition of 1893. The building that houses the museum was built in 1910 and was the administration building for the South Park Commission. The 46-year-old museum is scheduled to expand into an adjacent structure, the Roundhouse building, which will add 61,000 square feet of space. Both the north-entrance façade of the museum and the circular Roundhouse were designed by Burnham. The Roundhouse, formerly a horse stable, is a

Chicago Park District Historic Landmark.

Why I recommend visiting this site

DuSable Museum is one of the great museums dedicated to African-American history and culture. Visiting the museum is also a great excuse for visiting Washington Park, which is one of the exquisite parks designed by Frederick Law Olmsted and Calvert Vaux.

Highlights of the visit

When you enter the museum you are in Founders' Hall. This brightly lit, high-ceilinged space features mosaic portraits of the diverse group of museum founders by artist Thomas Miller, a Virginia-born visual artist and well-recognized painter. The founders include Dr. Margaret Burroughs,

Harold Washington wing

teacher, artist, and historian, who served as executive director from 1961–1985. Founders' Hall also features one of two busts of Jean Baptiste Point DuSable, the namesake of the museum, who is recognized as Chicago's first non-native

settler. DuSable's significance in Chicago history extends beyond his mere settlement and sojourn. He began an era of agrarian and commodities production in the region that helped Chicago become a center of commerce and

transportation.

The recently enhanced *Africa Speaks* exhibit includes beautifully displayed artifacts, masks, sculpture, jewelry, and multimedia interactive visual images that present the art and culture of African people from the

49

entire continent. One learns of the vast diversity of the world's second-largest continent and gains an appreciation for the connections that African people and nations have to the rest of the world. The curators have also explored the history of slavery and its impact on the culture and economic development of many countries, including the United States. Of particular interest is the Elmina Castle display. Also known as the Castle of Horror, Elmina was a Gold Coast fortress where, for hundreds of years, beginning in the 15th century and continuing with Dutch occupation in 1637, slaves were held captive before being loaded onto slave ships.

The Robert Witt Ames *Freedom Now* mural, housed in the small auditorium, is a beautifully detailed creation by Robert Witt Ames, a distinguished California sculptor and woodcrafter. This spectacular 9-foot by 8-foot wood-carved, bas-relief mural chronicles 400 years of the history of African peoples from their origins in Africa to the 1960s Civil Rights era. Ames depicts this history in 40 scenes, including those showing the Middle Passage, plantation workers in the fields and in their homes in the South, and Freedom School, which chronicles the voter registration efforts of the Civil Rights movement.

I guess I'm a sucker for the traditional, tried and true treasures in the

Burnham Roundhouse addition

permanent art gallery on the lower level. There is a small but powerful collection of paintings and sculptures by artists including Henry O. Tanner, Archibald Motley, William Artis, and Joseph Kersey.

Three things I learned

DuSable Museum has permanent galleries and collections as well as temporary exhibitions and attractions. Over the past few years, the museum has hosted a myriad of exhibitions of art and cultural information. These exhibitions include *Allen Stringfellow*; *120 Years of African-American Quilts*; *Annie Malone: Black Beauty Culture Pioneer and Millionaire*; *100 Plus One: Before Motown and Beyond*; *Harold Washington in Office*; and many more.

As is the case with most museums, DuSable has a gift shop. This one is called the *Tradin' Post*, a name that harkens back to the commercial business that DuSable engaged in with Native Americans and explorers in Chicago's early days. For those interested in Afro-centric books and art, Chicago history, and museum souvenirs, this shop is a real treasure.

When speaking with Antoinette Wright, the president of the DuSable Museum, about the museum's mission, she said, "Bernard, there's an African proverb that says 'Until the lion writes his own story, the tale will always glorify the hunter.' . . . When you visit the DuSable Museum of African-American History, we are charged with the pleasure of making sure that you experience and remember *our* story." That said it all to me.

Bernard C. Turner

Cardinal's mansion

Location

The tour group meets at the Chicago History Museum at North and Clark streets and walks approximately five blocks, primarily on Astor Street and inner Lake Shore Drive.

Description

The Gold Coast tour includes two blocks of Astor Street that have national landmark status, meaning that the buildings' facades cannot be changed. These buildings and those on other streets on the tour have not changed much since they were originally built.

Why I recommend visiting this site

Walking tours are great when the weather is fine: they allow you to see the sites as closely as possible. Walking these streets, you will have the same visual experience as that of well-to-do Chicagoans a hundred years ago. You can actually enter some of the buildings and get a sense of what life was like in the Gilded Age. The tour helps you discover why this particular area became Chicago's most fashionable neighborhood, and it explains the changes in land use and lifestyles that have taken place over the years.

Highlights of the visit

The Cardinal's residence at Astor Street and North Avenue is not only the first mansion built in the area, but it and the surrounding property and outbuildings have remained virtually unchanged since 1880. Because the property has continued to be used for its

Alfred F. Madlener House, home of Graham Foundation for fine arts

original purpose—a residence for the Catholic archdiocese—it is the only place where you can see what the entire neighborhood used to consist of: enormous ornate homes on large manicured lots stretching for entire blocks.

Arguably the most famous home in the area is the Charnley-Persky House at the corner of Astor and Schiller streets. This house, which is attributed to two of Chicago's most famous architects, Frank Lloyd Wright and Louis Sullivan, is known as the first "modern" house in America. People come from all over the world to take pictures of it. The house is now owned by the Society of Architectural Historians and is not open to the public except on a limited basis. Chicago History Museum walking tours are often invited in to view the main floor and hear the house's history.

The Museum and Headquarters of the International College of Surgeons at 1522 North Lake Shore Drive was originally the palatial home of the daughter of The Diamond Match Company's president, James Robinson, who built it for her as a wedding present. It is

Ambassador East Hotel

modeled on the Petit Trianon in Versailles and is one of the few original Lake Shore Drive mansions still standing. The staff always invites tour groups in for an introduction to the museum and a short visit.

Three things I learned

Why did this area become the place to live around the turn of the century? There are various events in Chicago history that helped to make the lakefront a major attraction: the removal of cemeteries from the area; the fire in 1871; and the influence of business leaders such as Potter Palmer. Previous to Palmer's building his mansion on Lake Shore Drive in 1882, Chicagoans did not think a lake view was desirable. Palmer made some of his fortune by buying up much of the area and building fashionable homes to be sold to only the best possible neighbors. He bought property at $60 a front foot and sold it a few years later at $1,200 a front foot.

The opening of the Michigan Avenue Bridge in 1920 doubled, and then tripled, North Side land values. Mansions began to come down and high-rise luxury co-ops and apartments began to go up. This was the first time the name "Gold Coast" was used, and the high-rise developers were known as prospectors. High-rise living was vogue in the 1920s, and building up allowed more people to live in a fashionable area. The area still boasts the most luxurious apartment towers in the city.

One of two remaining wooden alleys in the city is located in the Gold Coast one-half block south of North Avenue between Astor and State streets. The alley, which was built in 1909, is on the National Register of Historic Places.

It was paved with wooden blocks, a style that was once used extensively throughout the city. The decline in the Chicago lumber market coupled with a change to the tax assessment policies, led to a decrease in wood for street paving.

Suzanne Haynes

Graceland Cemetery

Clark Street and Irving Park Road

Daniel Burnham is buried on the small island on the right

Description

Graceland is the North Side's most important cemetery, both architecturally and historically. It was established in 1860 on what was then undeveloped land two miles north of Chicago's city limit. As the city grew north and west, it engulfed the cemetery.

Graceland originally took up 80 acres, but grew to 200 acres, and had the right to purchase up to 300 additional acres for burial grounds. Since the area was undeveloped, expansion plans did not initially meet with any opposition. But as people settled close to the land the cemetery held for expansion, local residents protested the idea of allowing the burial grounds to grow. Ultimately, the cemetery was confined to 120 acres.

Why I recommend visiting this site

Cemeteries can make people feel uncomfortable, but in the late 1800s Chicago's cemeteries were looked upon as parks. Before there were any significant parks in the city, people would picnic in and ride through Graceland Cemetery, enjoying its natural setting and beautiful landscaping. In fact, this was common at cemeteries around the world during the Victorian era.

Highlights of the visit

One surprising highlight was seeing a red fox streak across the green grass

Potter and Bertha Palmer lie at rest in twin sarcophagi in this Greek Temple.

during our tour. Not only was the fox strikingly elegant, but seeing a relatively exotic animal was a big surprise, given that we were in the middle of a big city. It made me realize that Graceland is a vast, open, bucolic space—an oasis for wildlife as well as a haven for those who have passed

away. What an attractive place for all to find peace and quiet, whether human or animal, dead or alive.

One thing that makes Graceland extraordinary is the many notable Chicagoans who are buried there. The list reads like a veritable Who's Who of Chicago's builders and

leaders: Kinzie, Palmer, Pullman, Field, McCormick, Armour, Burnham, Harrison, Pinkerton, etc. Some of their graves, decorated with columns, arches, and statues, were designed by the likes of Louis Sullivan and Mies van der Rohe, both of whom are also buried there.

I knew all that going in, but seeing the graves inspired me to learn more about these history makers. In addition, I learned a lot about Chicago through this tour. For example, Graceland includes thousands of graves of Civil War soldiers who had originally been buried at the City Cemetery at the southern end of what is now Lincoln Park. When City Cemetery was gradually closed, starting in the 1860s, the Confederate soldiers buried there were reinterred, ironically, on the South Side; the Union soldiers were reinterred on the North Side.

The Civil War is not the only human tragedy that landed people at Graceland. Victims of the Iroquois Theater fire, the *Eastland* disaster and the *Titanic*'s sinking are buried there. Interestingly, no victims of the Great Chicago Fire were buried at Graceland.

Three things I learned

Graceland was built on high ground, which makes it appropriate for burials. What is now Clark Street was once the shore of Lake Michigan. As the lake receded thousands of years ago, it left a series of ridges and swales, many of which can still be seen in the local topography. The high ground was used for roads, as well as for the cemetery.

At one time it was common for cemeteries to surround family plots with low stone walls, iron railings, or hedges. Such was the case with about 50 acres at Graceland. Eventually this area was opened up, and

Beautiful and serene, Graceland Cemetery was once a popular picnic spot.

Graceland assumed its tranquil, park-like setting.

A big baseball serves as the monument for William Hulbert, the founder of the National League of Professional Baseball Clubs in 1876. One of the original eight teams listed on the monument was the Chicago White Stockings, a team that became the Cubs and now plays a few blocks south of the cemetery at Wrigley Field.

Greg Borzo

Green Line 'L' South

The 'L' passes through the tunnel over the Illinois Institute of Technology's student center.

Description

The nation's first elevated transit line was built in New York in 1867. Although Chicagoans talked for decades about catching up with their East Coast rival, it took the World's Columbian Exposition of 1893 to motivate the city to build an elevated of its own. Transportation was a big part of the city's proposal to Congress for the exposition, especially once a site far from downtown hotels and railroad stations was selected.

The South Side Rapid Transit began operating in 1892 between Congress and 39th Street, but was quickly extended south to the exposition, reaching the site a few days after it opened.

The exposition attracted almost 26 million people—at a time when the population of the United States was 52 million people—and confirmed Chicago as a trend setting, world-class city.

Why I recommend visiting this site

This was Chicago's first elevated transit rail line. Except for renovations in 1994–96, the line has been running 24 hours a day, seven days a week, ever since it was opened in 1892. A tour offered once a month on the "Alley L" by the Chicago History Museum (CHM) is the best way to experience this irresistible ride through history.

The CHM tour is a Four Star happening—not only because it is so good, but also because it travels past and touches on all the sites that are represented by the four stars on the Chicago flag. The tour starts near the site of Fort Dearborn, which, when built in 1803, was the United States' westernmost fort; it rides through the path of the Great Chicago Fire of 1871, which started near DeKoven and Jefferson streets and burned all the way north to Fullerton Avenue; it passes by the site of the 1933 Century of Progress; and it

The 1892 station house at Garfield, one of the oldest mass transit stations in the country.

ends near Jackson Park, where the World's Columbian Exposition was held.

Highlights of the visit

Chicago grew up, as a city, on the South Side, and the Green Line traces that growth. As the train heads south, it passes many interesting places: railroad yards and warehouses; Printer's Row (an old printing district still known for great bookstores); the Levy, which was once an infamous vice district; Prairie Avenue Historical District (Chicago's first Gold Coast); the Black Belt (a narrow stretch of land where African-Americans who came to Chicago in the Great Migration were once confined to live); interstate highways; a baseball park (home of the Chicago White Sox, winners of the 2005 World Series); the stock-yards (once a major tourist attraction); Washington Park (landscaped by Fredrick Law Olmsted); 63rd Street, the street where *The Devil in the White City*, a.k.a. Henry Holmes, lived; and several universities.

Along the train's route you can feel the development of the dynamic city roll out before you, as ethnic groups came and went, churches and synagogues changed ownership, poverty blighted the area with vacant lots, historical sites were lost ... or preserved, and as neighborhoods continue to be reborn.

Three things I learned

Some of Chicago's oldest buildings abut the Green Line downtown and immediately south of the Loop. They were built right after the Great Chicago Fire

The last Stateway Gardens high-rise peers out from behind the 'L' structure at 35th and State.

of 1871 and are still standing because for decades the elevated structure depressed the value of adjacent property—inadvertently protecting the old buildings along its right-of-way. Today, the rejuvenation of the Loop and construction of the new Millennium Park have caused property values in the area to skyrocket. Alas, this means that many of these buildings are being torn down.

The Green Line and its precursors changed dramatically over time. Seven of the original nine stations between Congress and 39th streets have been closed due to low ridership. Also, three stations at the end of the line have been lopped off. Meanwhile, branch lines to the Stockyards and Kenwood have come and gone. Ridership on the Green Line is poised to bounce back, however, as the neighborhoods it serves are revitalized.

Initially, Green Line cars were pulled by small steam locomotives—veritable "Little Engines that Could!" In 1898, however, the service was converted to the current system of electrical power drawn from a third rail. This technology was proven on a small elevated train circuit that carried people around at the World's Columbian Exposition fairgrounds. The innovative electric ride/people mover was high-tech at the time and successfully carried more than six million fairgoers—setting a design and technology precedent for all of Chicago's 'L' lines.

Greg Borzo

Green Line 'L' West

Golden-domed Garfield Park Fieldhouse

Location

One of several popular 'L' tours offered by the Chicago History Museum, the Green Line/Lake Street 'L' tour highlights the second oldest line in the system. The tour begins at the Clark Street/Lake Street station, a hub that connects the Blue, Orange, Green, Brown, and Purple Lines, a "super station," the busiest in the Loop. The station, across from the Thompson Center is tri-level, with access to the Blue Line subway and to the Loop lines.

Description

The tour takes about an hour and a half, disembarking at the Garfield Park

Conservatory, Oak Park, and the Clinton Street station. This station is named for DeWitt Clinton, the former New York mayor and governor famous for developing the Erie Canal. This is significant for Chicago's history because the canal contributed to the city's development as a transportation hub.

Why I recommend visiting this site

Originally called the Lake Street Line—incorporated in 1888 and opened in November 1893—the Green Line 'L' currently travels from Harlem Avenue/Lake to either Cottage Grove Avenue/East 63rd Street or to Ashland Avenue/63rd in Englewood. This tour focuses on the route to Harlem/Lake in Oak Park

and back, although at its inception, the service was between Madison Street and Market (today's Wacker Drive) and California Avenue. What's significant about this line is that, in an expanding city, people living outside of what is now

downtown Chicago could travel to and from the business district, which was originally along Lake Street.

Highlights of the visit

One can look at the Green Line/Lake Street 'L' line's route and surmise that

there have been significant changes to the landscape over the years. There are, frankly, "blank spaces" on the route. Just as in other parts of the city, new businesses, new housing, and new attractions will soon be evident along the line. The

Garfield Park Conservatory

sights that appeal to me are the gorgeous views of the Chicago River as you go west past the Merchandise Mart, the absolutely magnificent Garfield Park and its field house, the beautiful and tranquil Conservatory, and the allure of Oak Park.

What occurred to me while traveling past the Merchandise Mart and looking at the river was that this was like viewing a map. At one point you can see all three branches of the Chicago River as it goes from east to west, then north and south. The Merchandise Mart is also impressive; most impressive when it is lit up at night. Still possibly the largest commercial building in the world, the Mart has 4.2 million square feet of space and features design,

furniture, and shopping venues.

The swift car whisks you past several transporta-

suburban Metra trains and Union Station for both Metra and long-distance Amtrak service.

Greenhouse at Conservatory

tion hubs on Clinton Street, including the Ogilvie Transportation Center for

After the train passes Kedzie Avenue, named for a contemporary of Abraham

Lincoln and another outspoken opponent of slavery, you reach Garfield Park. Like other important

parks in a city whose motto is *urbs in horto* (city in a garden), Garfield Park was

65

designed by a well-known landscape designer, William LeBaron Jenney, in 1874. One of the three oldest West Side parks, Garfield rivals Douglas and Humboldt parks in size and beauty. One of the highlights is the field house with its golden dome and the Conservatory a couple of blocks north, built in 1907 by landscape architect, Jens Jensen. This is a stopping-off point on the tour. The Conservatory is at once beautiful and comforting, especially in winter. It's a lush, green, tropical paradise you'll want to visit again and again.

The train leaves the city limits at Austin Avenue (6000 West) and enters Oak Park. Besides being a pleasant, diverse and historically significant suburb, Oak Park is home to the architecture of Frank Lloyd Wright, whose work here consists of 25 homes and his studio. The train passes beautiful parks and homes and Oak Park-River Forest High School, where Ernest Hemingway once wrote for the school newspaper.

Three things I learned

As is the case with the other 'L' lines, the developers had to obtain rights from landowners and businessmen. One curiosity of the Green Line is that some of the supports for the elevated tracks are on the sidewalk and some supports east of Western Avenue are in the street. In Oak Park, the tracks run parallel to the Union Pacific Railway tracks.

At the Ashland Avenue station you get a view of the Lyon and Healy building, which the company has occupied since 1899. This venerable Chicago business began in 1864 as a music publishing company, but later produced musical instruments. Today, Lyon and Healy is one of the few companies worldwide that manufactures harps.

Ashland Avenue was originally named Reuben Street, for real estate developer Reuben Taylor, but was later renamed Ashland Avenue for the Kentucky estate of Henry Clay, Speaker of the House of Representatives in the early 1800s. Taylor's wife, however, does have a street named after her—Paulina Street.

The Paulina Connector Bridge is what remains of the Lake Street Transfer from the Lake Street Elevated to the Metropolitan, now the Blue Line. It was operational from 1913–1951 and will now be part of the new Pink Line that goes to Pilsen and back to the Loop.

Bernard C. Turner

Haymarket Square

Randolph and Des Plaines Street

Mary Brogger's sculpture of workers holding speakers up on a wagon was erected in 2004.

Description

The Haymarket Square story is told in greater detail elsewhere, but here are a few key events. May 1, 1886: The Knights of Labor called a nationwide strike to support demands for an eight-hour working day.

May 3: Strikers at Cyrus McCormick's International Harvester factory in Chicago fought with strikebreakers and police, resulting in several deaths.

May 4: Workers gathered at Haymarket Square. When police charged the workers, someone threw a bomb, which killed several policemen. The police fired, killing several workers and probably several policemen as well.

Eight labor organizers, most of whom were foreigners, but none of whom were proven to have thrown the bomb, were convicted for the deed and found guilty. Four of them were executed, and one committed suicide to avoid the hangman's noose.

The tour guide discussed the socio-political forces that led up to this tragedy. Business leaders, who exploited labor in this laissez faire period, regarded the labor movement as a threat to the status quo. The public saw labor leaders as anarchists and atheists. Newspapers fanned the fires. Politicians acquiesced.

Why I recommend visiting this site

While traveling in Europe years ago, I learned that many Europeans think of Chicago in terms of three things: Al Capone, the Stockyards (which used to be a major tourist attraction), and the Haymarket Square bombing.

What was that last one again? I was born in Chicago but barely knew a thing about it! Time to check it out, and what better way than the Chicago History Museum's Haymarket Square bus tour, typically offered every year in May.

The bombing is famous, I learned, because it is the reason Labor Day is celebrated in May all around the world. Everywhere except the United States, that is. America—in particular, Chicago—has always tried to deflect attention from the shameful incident in which eight people were wrongfully

Louis Lingg, one of the Haymarket martyrs, lived here, at 1544 N. Sedgwick Street.

convicted of—and five of them died for—throwing a bomb at a group of policemen. But history will not let us forget.

Highlights of the visit

The best part of this tour was to visit—to actually stand at—the very locations where the

Haymarket Square bomb went off and where innocent men were imprisoned, tried, executed, and buried. It was chilling, especially these days, when news reports make it so clear that capital punishment is often wrongfully implemented.

The bus tour included stops at Haymarket Square (on Randolph Street between Des Plaines and Halsted streets); the Cook County Criminal Courts Building, where the trial took place; the nearby site where the Haymarket Square martyrs were held and then hung; and Waldheim Cemetery (in Forest Park), where many of them were buried.

This tour is great because it is so comprehensive. Along the way to Haymarket Square, we passed sites where some of the convicted had lived. We visited other places in the area immediately surrounding the place where the bombing occurred, including meeting halls and the former site of the station where the police had gathered. We visited labor history sites, mansions, and monuments.

At the cemetery, we learned about Lucy Parsons, a labor organizer and activist of African-American, Native-American, and Mexican ancestry. Parsons fought against poverty, racism, and the excesses of capitalism. After her husband, Albert Parsons, was hung for the bombing, Lucy spoke out about the injustice. The cemetery is also the site of the grave of Emma Goldman, an anarchist and feminist, and of the ashes of Joe Hill, a union organizer.

In 2004, a monument honoring the martyrs was finally erected at Haymarket Square: It features a 15-foot speaker's wagon, in memory of the wagon from which labor leaders spoke on that fateful evening in 1886. This bronze sculpture by Mary Brogger also makes a statement about free speech.

Visiting Haymarket Square and other sites connected to the incident was moving and made the people and events more memorable than just reading about them in a book such as this one, so go and experience the place for yourself.

Three things I learned

This event marks the first time dynamite was used in peacetime in this country, and it terrified Americans.

In response, Fort Sheridan was built to quell anticipated labor violence, and LaSalle Avenue was widened to facilitate the movement of troops through the city.

The bombing and its aftermath halted a burgeoning labor movement in the United States.

In 1899, a statue of a policeman raising a hand to restore order was erected in the square in commemoration of the bombing. In 1969, and again in 1970, the statue was bombed off its pedestal by modern-day activists. As a result, it was relocated to police headquarters at 1121 South State Street. The statue now stands in the police academy at 1300 West Jackson Boulevard.

Greg Borzo

69

Holy Family Church

1019 South May

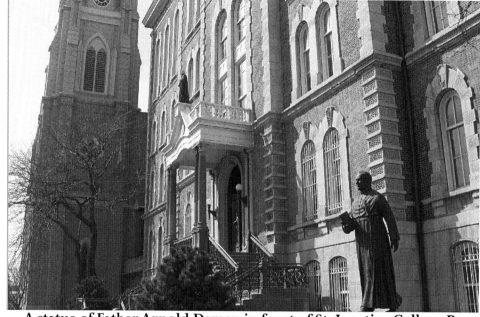

A statue of Father Arnold Damen in front of St. Ignatius College Prep and Holy Family Church (left)

Description

Holy Family is Chicago's second oldest church (the oldest one being the much better known Old St. Patrick's at 140 South Des Plaines Street). Construction of Holy Family began in 1857 and continued through 1874, when the upper steeple was finished. When it was officially opened in 1860, the area around the church at the outskirts of the city was sparsely populated. Holy Family quickly attracted a large congregation, mostly of Irish immigrants, but also Germans and Bohemians.

Why I recommend visiting this site

Years ago, I heard a story that this church

was spared by the Great Chicago Fire of 1871, which started a few blocks away, because Father Arnold Damen invoked the aid of Our Lady of Perpetual Help to save the building. I was drawn by this legend of a "Miracle on Roosevelt Road" to learn more about the church.

In all likelihood, I found out, the priest's prayers came too late to have had any impact on the fire, since he was in New York City when the conflagration started and received news of the fire by telegram. In any event, in his prayers Damen promised that if his church were saved he would light seven perpetual vigil lights. Those lights burn to this day inside the church (although they are now electric bulbs rather than candles), in front of a painting of Our Lady of Perpetual Help.

Highlights of the visit

One of the highlights of the tour was discovering the historical importance of this little-known church: It is one of the few public buildings left standing after the Great Chicago Fire of 1871.

The structure is one of the best examples of a German Gothic church in the United States. Notable features include the following: 15,000 square feet of space with seating for 1,000; a 65-foot-high ceiling throughout the sanctuary; 12 Tiffany windows, the oldest stained-glass windows in Chicago; a world-class pipe organ from 1870 that made the church a popular place

Until 1889, Holy Family's 230-foot tower was the tallest structure in Chicago.

for musical performances; and an ornate, 230-foot-tall bell tower, once the tallest structure in Chicago.

By 1890, Holy Family had become the largest English-speaking parish in the United States, with more than 25,000 parishioners. Over the years, however, the neighborhood declined. By 1984, the size of the congregation had dwindled so much that the church was closed.

Thanks to the efforts of the Holy Family Preservation Society, the church survived this calamity. The wrecker's ball threatened again in 1990, but the building was saved through another massive fundraising effort, this time producing enough money to actually restore the edifice. Restoration took from 1991 to 2002, but now the church's future is assured, despite the fact that the building is somewhat worn by time.

St. Ignatius College Prep, one of the city's elite private high schools and the forerunner of Loyola University, is situated next door to the church, at 1076 West Roosevelt Road. The school was founded in 1869 as St. Ignatius College, which makes this Chicago's oldest school still in operation. The architectural style is decidedly French. Typical of many 19th-century schools, the assembly room or library is on the top floor, where it is structurally easier to include a high ceiling.

Both the church and school were founded by Father Damen, a remarkable, energetic man. Born in Holland in 1815, he was appointed the first pastor of St. Francis Xavier Church in St. Louis in 1844, when Chicago was still a pioneer town. He conducted a mission in Chicago in 1856 and was invited to come back as a priest at Holy Name Church on State and Superior streets.

More adventuresome than that, Damen decided instead to build his own parish at what was then the edge of town, and he succeeded admirably. Father Arnold Damen, S.J., founder of a big church on the prairie, died in 1890.

Three things I learned

Patrick and Catherine O'Leary, owners of Chicago's most famous cow, were once parishioners of Holy Family. The Great Chicago Fire of 1871 started at DeKoven and Jefferson streets, just four blocks east of the church, but the winds swept the fire in the other direction.

The top floor of St. Ignatius College Prep was originally used as a natural history museum. Today the only such museum on Roosevelt Road is the Field Museum, two miles to the east.

Damen Avenue, formerly Robey Street, was officially renamed in honor of Father Arnold Damen in 1927.

Greg Borzo

Café Brauer is a classic example of the Prairie School of design.

Description

Parks in Chicago date back to the 1850s. Early parks were typically small and full of weeds, garbage, and grazing animals. The city did not get serious about parks until 1869, when Illinois established three park commissions in Chicago and allocated sufficient funds to develop and maintain parks.

When the North Park Commission set to work, one of their first tasks was to clear away a cemetery! From 1842 to the 1870s, the southern tip of what is now Lincoln Park was City Cemetery. Burying people in sandy soil so close to the city's water supply, however, contributed to outbreaks of cholera and other diseases, so the bodies were reinterred elsewhere. No one knows why, but one burial vault—the Couch Tomb—remains, just north of the Chicago History Museum.

The park grew, bit by bit, to encompass six miles of shoreline and 1,212 acres, stretching from Oak Street to Ardmore Avenue. Today it comprises many features, including the following: a one-quarter-mile-long European style mall lined with trees; formal French-style flower gardens next to an informal plot of perennials and wildflowers; a waterfowl pond; a bird sanctuary; areas landscaped with local plants; a zoo; a golf course; baseball fields; tennis courts; and six beaches; as well as sailing, swan, and crew boats.

Why I recommend visiting this site

After reading in the newspaper that more than 17 million people visit Lincoln Park every year, I just had to learn more about it. What makes the park such a popular playground, urban oasis, historical treasure, and nature refuge?

Also, besides being the city's biggest and busiest park, Lincoln Park is the home of the Chicago History Museum. That's all the more reason to check it out.

Highlights of the visit

I expected to see trees, flowers, and beautiful views of Lake Michigan, so I was surprised to discover the many beautiful statues scattered throughout the park (all of them south of Addison Street). Following

People often sit on Shakespeare's lap for a photo.

are a few of the more remarkable ones, from south to north.

• Standing Abraham Lincoln

(1887) is very realistic because the face was created from a life mask of Lincoln made in 1860. It is set along what was once a stylish carriage drive.

- Ben Franklin (1896) was built with funds from the Old Printers Association of Chicago and Joseph Medill, an editor of the *Chicago Tribune*. Although Franklin was a scientist and statesman, this unpretentious statue commemorates his accomplishments as a printer.

- Ulysses S. Grant (1891) is erected on a colossal Romanesque base with funds generated by a public subscription campaign organized by Potter Palmer, a civic leader, and Joseph Stockton, a Civil War general.

- William Shakespeare (1893) was created for the World's Columbian Exposition. The Bard of Avon is seated serenely,

Several plaques mark ridges in the park that were once the shoreline of Lake Michigan.

low enough to the ground for visitors to sit on his lap.

Buildings in the park include a world-class conservatory, built in 1894 and modeled after the magnificent Crystal Palace at the World's Fair of 1851 in Hyde Park, London, and the beautiful Café Brauer, a masterpiece of the Prairie School style, which was built in 1908 and now houses a restaurant and other facilities open to the public.

Three things I learned

In 1878, a "floating hospital" was opened on the lake at North Avenue. It provided fresh air, rest, and wholesome food for up to 5,000 mothers and children seeking refuge from Chicago's grime and polluted air. In 1890, a similar fresh air sanitarium opened at Fullerton Avenue. That building today serves as the Chicago Park District's Theater on the Lake.

Bicycles were not officially allowed in the park until 1882. They were considered speed demons, limited to eight miles per hour, while horses were limited to six miles per hour. In fact, roads in the park and in Chicago itself were originally paved to accommodate bicycle traffic—long before automobiles joined the scene. During the bicycle craze of the 1890s, Chicago had more than 200 bicycle clubs, many of which rode through Lincoln Park.

Bronze markers scattered around the south end of the park mark the changing shoreline of Lake Michigan. Thousands of years ago, retreating glaciers formed the lake. As they moved and melted, the glaciers left a series of ridges and swales. Many ridges were used to make roads, including Clark Street. Although the park was covered with topsoil, the underlying, rolling topography can still be seen.

Greg Borzo

Explore
Lincoln Park
Neighborhood

McCormick Row Houses

Location

The borders of the Lincoln Park neighborhood are Diversey Parkway and North Avenue on the north and south, respectively, Lake Michigan on the east, and Clybourn Avenue on the west. Basically, it's the neighborhood just west of the Lincoln Park Zoo.

Description

Lincoln Park is now considered one of the more wealthy neighborhoods in the city. Many examples of fine architecture can be found in the area, including the town houses on Fullerton Parkway between Clark and Orchard streets, the ornate Beaux Art Dewes Mansion at 503 West

Wrightwood Avenue, the Chicago Landmark Reebie Storage Warehouse at 2325 North Clark Street, and the Elks National Memorial on Lakeview Avenue and Diversey Parkway.

Lincoln Park is a good example of how a neighborhood changes demographically, economically, and aesthetically over time. Now on the high end of the socio-economic scale, with expensive homes and condominiums, the neighborhood bounced back from decline during the Depression. Due to the efforts of organizations such as the Lincoln Park Conservation Association, the neighborhood achieved urban renewal through property rehabilitation, with the aid of federal funding and the enforcement of housing codes.

Why I recommend visiting this site

The diversity of Chicago's neighborhoods contributes to the charm and greatness of the city. Lincoln Park is just one of the wonderful neighborhoods that are perfect for strolling and enjoying the architecture and ambience.

As revealed by the informative walking tour offered by the Chicago History Museum, this neighborhood demonstrates how architecture, businesses, and civic and social institutions serve to teach about and illuminate Chicago history and culture.

Highlights of the visit

Touring the DePaul University campus and learning about the history of the McCormick Theological Seminary and the McCormick Row Houses was the most interesting part of the visit. The McCormick Theological Seminary was originally

Cortelyou Commons, DePaul University

founded at Hanover College in Indiana. Later, due to economic problems, the seminary moved to Chicago in order to receive financial backing from the wealthy reaper manufacturer, Cyrus McCormick. After it moved to Chicago, the school was renamed the Presbyterian Seminary of the Northwest, but was again renamed for McCormick when he died in 1886.

Beginning in 1882, a series of row houses intended for middle-income families was built as a way of generating income to supplement McCormick's endowment. This venture proved to be so successful that additional homes were constructed on Fullerton and Belden avenues and on Chalmers Place. As with many houses in post-fire Chicago, the McCormick row houses were designed by well-known architects in a style reminiscent of the Queen Anne-style houses that were popular in industrial-age America. The design of these houses, however, was less decorative and ornate than that of Queen Anne homes in other cities and in other Chicago neighborhoods, such as Old Town.

The seminary eventually became affiliated with the University of Chicago and moved to Hyde Park. The move enabled DePaul University to purchase the McCormick campus during the years 1975 to 1976. Many of the buildings that belonged to the seminary were demolished during the urban renewal period of the 1960s. Many of the row houses, however, are still standing.

One of the most beautiful buildings on the DePaul campus, facing the Chalmers row houses, is the Gothic revival Cortelyou

Egyptian style architecture on Reebie Storage building on Clark Street

Commons building. Although it was originally part of the seminary's plan to have all of its buildings rebuilt in this style, this is the only one remaining. The other completed building, the Waterman Gymnasium, built in 1929, was recently demolished as part of the Brown Line elevated train renovation.

Three things I learned

Lincoln Park originally only extended as far as Fullerton Avenue. The town just north was Lake View, which extended all the way to Evanston. In 1889, the City of Chicago expanded and annexed Lake View, giving the land north of Fullerton to Lincoln Park.

Clybourn Avenue, on the western edge of Lincoln Park, is named after Archibald Clybourn, the first man to build a Chicago stockyard, in 1829. Clybourn and his father were butchers, and their stockyard and meat slaughtering business paved the way for many more to come, culminating in the famous Union Stockyards, which opened in 1865 and consolidated several stockyards scattered around the city.

DePaul University is the largest Roman Catholic university in the United States and one of the 10 largest private institutions of higher learning. Focusing on teaching and service to the community, DePaul has six campuses, including the Lincoln Park and Loop campuses, as well as suburban campuses in Rolling Meadows and Naperville.

Bernard C. Turner

Marshall Field's

111 North State Street

Marshall Field's Atrium with American flag

Description

Marshall Field (1835–1906) was a great American success story. He started out as a clerk and became the owner of one of the most famous and recognized retail establishments in the world. In 1864, Field and a partner, Levi Leiter, joined Potter Palmer in the dry goods business. Palmer retired in 1868, and in 1881 Field bought out his remaining partner and changed the store's name to Marshall Field and Company. This name remained until the fall of 2006 when the store was sold and renamed Macy's. Marshall Field's current State Street store was designed by the architectural firm of D.H. Burnham & Company. In 1978, the building was designated a National Historic Landmark, both for its beauty and for its historical significance.

Why I recommend visiting this site:

Field was a major influence in Chicago becoming a world-class city. His legacy is evident in places such as the Art Institute, the Field Museum, and the University of Chicago. His most famous quote—and evidence of how he became a success— was, "Give the lady what she wants." It is clear that he also helped define for the lady what it was that she wanted.

This department store is one of only two in the United States (possibly in the world) that is so special that it has an archivist on

Marshall Field's clock

staff. While the store epitomizes what shopping is—and most people come here for that purpose—it is interesting that many people come on a mission and start looking, not for things to buy in this building, but for

things to see. Its worldwide reputation is evident in that many of these visitors are from other countries and can be seen looking up, searching for the Tiffany ceiling.

Self-guided audio tours

are available here any time during store hours.

Highlights of the visit

The Archive on the seventh floor contains an extensive collection of items from the 150 years the store

82

Washington Street view of Marshall Field's

has been in existence. Treasures from the store's past include 19th-century perfume bottles, women's shoes and opera glasses made especially for Field's, and photos of various looks the store has sported over the years.

The great green clocks located on the exterior of the building at State and Washington streets and State and Randolph streets, weighing in at more than seven tons each, have kept Chicago on time for more than a century. Norman Rockwell did a famous painting of the Great Clock that appeared on the cover of *The Saturday Evening Post* in 1945. Almost every Chicagoan has made plans to meet someone under one of these clocks at some time in their life. If there is ever a question as to where the store is located, the clocks are the obvious giveaway. Green, incidentally, is the store's signature color.

The Tiffany Ceiling on the fifth floor, built in 1907, is the largest unbroken example of Tiffany Favrile glass in the world, containing more than 1.6 million pieces. This vaulted ceiling can be seen from the ground floor by looking up from the cosmetic counter area (currently the Esteé Lauder or Lancôme coun-ters). For a closer look, go to Lingerie on the fifth floor.

The building is a major hub of the Loop Pedway System and leads directly into the subway station.

Three things I learned

Frango Mints are Marshall Field's signature candies. Not only were they exclusively sold at Field's stores but also they were once made on site at State Street. Although the store is 13 stories high, only 10 floors are used for retail. The candy was made on one of the upper floors. These floors, as well as other behind-the-scenes areas can be viewed during the public tours available on Saturdays.

The exterior of the building has as many interesting details as the interior. Besides the clocks, there are two enormous granite pillars at the State Street entrance. These were installed in 1902, and only the pillars on the Temple of Karnak in Egypt are taller. We are often so overwhelmed by the hustle and bustle of downtown that we don't notice even large and obvious features. I wasn't aware of these pillars until they were pointed out to me.

Every year a two-story Christmas tree is installed in the seventh-floor Walnut Room dining area and can be viewed from the eighth floor as well. Parents have been bringing their children to the beautiful Walnut Room for high tea for generations. At Christmas, lines of families with dressed-up children queue up here for lunch on their seasonal visit to see the great Christmas window displays. It is amazing that a department store can become such a part of our memory and tradition.

Suzanne Haynes

National Museum of Mexican Art
1852 West 19th Street

National Museum of Mexican Art

Location

The museum is located in the heart of the Pilsen area, which is west of Canal Street, south of 16th Street, east of Damen Avenue and north of the Chicago River. The Dan Ryan and Stevenson expressways intersect at East Pilsen.

Description

The National Museum of Mexican Art was founded in 1982 as the Mexican Fine Arts Center Museum. It contains primarily fine art but has evolved to include performing arts space, a radio station, and historical exhibits. The museum promotes Hispanic films, writers, and performance artists. While primarily committed to Mexican culture, it is the go-to place for all the wealth and breadth of Latino culture in Chicago.

Why I recommend visiting this site

Chicago is made up of neighborhoods of diverse cultures. In order to discover all her treasures, you need to get off the beaten path.

The migration of Mexican Americans started to take shape in Pilsen about 1964, making it amazing that a museum of the stature of The National Museum of Mexican Art was developed there by 1982.

Mexicans came to Chicago for the same reason as most other immigrants— in search of work. Because many worked on the railroads, they often came through Chicago and, until recently, Chicago offered them some of the highest wages in the United States. As these workers returned to Mexico with modern goods and ideas, they shared their experiences with others. It wasn't just the things they brought back, though; it was *la aventura*—the experience of Chicago—that encouraged others to come here. The museum carries on this tradition of providing visitors with yet one more unique experience.

Admission to the museum is free, but donations are accepted.

Highlights of the visit

The exhibit area consists of five major sections that follow the history of Mexican culture chronologically, beginning

Museum design with Aztec features

with The Pre-Cuauhtémoc Era and ending with The Mexican Experience in the United States.

The whole neighborhood was part of our experience, as the museum is in the heart of the Mexican community. Take time to window shop at unusual stores on bustling 18th Street and get a recommendation from the museum staff for places to eat. The prices are great and the food more authentic than that you will find in Mexican restaurants in other parts of town.

Today, the Pilsen community is 70 percent Hispanic and has the largest Mexican population in the city. The area was originally settled by Bohemians and Czechoslovakians, and, in 1870, it was called Little Pilsen, after a major Czech city. Prior to that, as early as the days of Marquette and Joliet, it was a crossroads of activity for those coming into the community and was once referred to as Port of Entry.

You might want your visit to include other Pilsen landmarks, such as Thalia Hall on 18th Street, which was designated a Chicago landmark in 1989. Built as a hall for meetings and musical theatrical productions, it is unique, due to its interior theater, which was modeled after that of the Old Opera House in Prague, Czechoslovakia.

Three things I learned

The National Museum of Mexican Art is one of the most highly accredited of its type in the country and even sponsors traveling exhibits in the national and international arena. It is the first and only Latino museum in the country accredited by the American Association of Museums.

In addition to its impressive collection of classical and contemporary Mexican art, the museum has an ambitious schedule of programs. These include an annual Día de los Muertos (Day of the Dead) celebration, readings by award winning authors such

Modern Art exhibition painting

as Octavio Paz and Carlos Fuentes, and performances by well-known musicians.

The museum collaborates with other organizations to present the Chicago International Latino Cinema Festival and has presented premiers of many Latino films, particularly those related to the arts.

Suzanne Haynes

Moody Bible Institute and Church

Institute: 820 North
LaSalle Drive

Church: North Avenue
and Clark Street

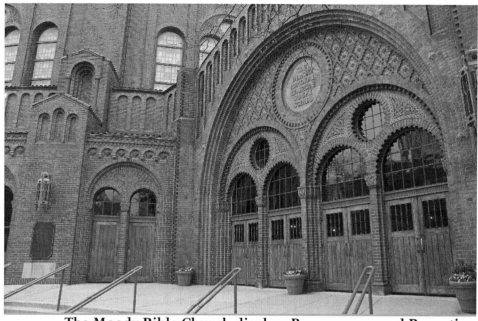

The Moody Bible Church displays Romanesque and Byzantine architectural styles.

Description

Both the Moody Bible Institute and the Moody Church have deep historic roots in Chicago. The church and its works are known around the world. With 26 acres between Chicago Avenue and Oak Street, the Moody Bible Institute is the largest landowner in the center of Chicago.

The church and the institute are separate entities, although both were founded by Dwight L. Moody (1837–1899). Before the days of Billy Sunday or Billy Graham, there was Moody. He was a charismatic leader and a spellbinding preacher. Over his lifetime, Moody preached—in

Explore

person—to more than 100 million people.

The Institute contains a museum (open Monday–Saturday) that includes displays about the organization, as well as a video about the life and ministries of Dwight L. Moody.

Why I recommend visiting this site

My interest in learning about the Moody Bible Institute stems from hearing several times on the evening news that the school's athletic facility serves as a practice site for opponents of the Chicago Bulls. Providing visiting pro teams free use of its sports complex, I learned on our tour, is typical of how Moody gives back to the community—whether it's offering people a home-away-from-home, helping inner-city kids meet their potential, or providing spiritual guidance to all who seek it.

Highlights of the visit

One highlight of our visit was learning how vast the Moody organization is. Moody started his congregation in 1864, when he founded the Illinois Street Church. From the beginning, Moody focused his ministry on the poor, the homeless, orphans, and city dwellers. Today the nondenominational, evangelical organization thrives and runs a number of services and programs around Chicago. It also has about 60 missionaries around the world.

The current church at Clark Street and North Avenue was dedicated in

Student center at the Moody Bible Institute.

1925. The architectural styles found in the massive red brick building are Romanesque and Byzantine. The exterior is patterned after the Church of Holy Wisdom in Istanbul, and the interior is light and spacious.

The Moody Bible Institute, primarily a university, was founded in 1886. Today it employs more than 700 people and trains some 1,800 students (about three-fourths of whom are undergraduates) to become pastors, teachers, missionaries, pilots, evangelists, musicians, and more.

The school is innovative. In 1926, it launched WMBI-AM, which made it a pioneer in evangelical broadcasting. Today, the institute owns and operates more than 30 noncommercial, ministry-focused stations around the country. In 1946, the school established the first missionary flight program in the country. The training is vital, because many missionaries practice in remote areas that are virtually inaccessible by road or water.

Moody is so successful that it does not charge tuition. As a result, it only accepts about 30 percent of its applicants.

Three things I learned

Dwight Moody was related to Harriet Beecher Stowe, Oliver Wendell Holmes, Grover Cleveland, and Franklin D. Roosevelt. He also played an important role in launching the YMCA, serving for a time as its president.

The first superintendent of the Bible Institute of the Chicago Evangelistic Society, which later became the Moody Bible Institute, was Reuben Archer Torrey. In memory of him, to this day, Moody's sports teams are known as the Arches. In addition, the school's symbol is an arch, of which there are plenty around the campus.

In 1860, Abraham Lincoln visited Moody's popular Sunday School on his way to his first inauguration in Washington, D.C. The Sunday school typically attracted more than 1,000 people every week, making it the largest mission of its kind in Chicago at that time.

Greg Borzo

Oak Woods Cemetery

1035 East 67th Street
Located in the Grand
Crossing community

Confederate Mound

Description

Oak Woods is the largest and most important cemetery located on the South Side of Chicago. It was established in 1854 on land outside of the city limits. Later, this and other neighboring areas such as Hyde Park were annexed and became part of Chicago. While several of the lovely major Chicago parks such as Jackson Park, Washington Park, and Douglas Park were designed by Frederic Law Olmsted, Oak Woods's design was conceived by another well-known landscape designer, Adolph Strauch. His work influenced Olmsted, who designed cemeteries such as the Mountain View

91

cemetery in Oakland, California.

Oak Woods was developed on 180 acres of land owned by Marcus Farwell. It is really an interment park with trees and lakes. Over the years there have been 188,000 thousand burials in the cemetery.

Why I recommend visiting this site

If you want to know something about the character and history of a city, visit its oldest graveyards. Chicago's graveyards are some of the most historic and scenic in the country. In addition to Oak Woods on the South Side, there are Graceland, Rose Hill and Bohemian National cemeteries on the North Side. All are the burial places of noteworthy

Old English Chapel with 9-11 Memorial in foreground

Chicagoans and help to illustrate the important role that the City of Chicago plays in American history.

Highlights of the visit

Entering Oak Woods is like entering an enclosed forest. Adding beauty to the tree-filled landscape are a series of smaller lakes and a larger one called Symphony Lake. Several Chicago mayors are buried in this prestigious area of the graveyard park. The area of the south wall that is bordered by 71st Street was the Jewish Oak Woods cemetery. It is no longer a separate entity.

The beauty and grandeur of the tombs and graves of the rich and

Harold Washington Tomb

famous is the best and most interesting aspect of Oak Woods. Many of the intricate aboveground tombs were designed by the famous architects of the day, as were those in Graceland Cemetery.

Among Chicago mayors buried here are William Hale "Big Bill" Thompson, the reputedly crooked mayor who was in office during the Capone era, and Harold Washington, the first African-American mayor.

Another revered Chicago leader buried in Oak Woods is Bishop Louis Henry Ford, founder of the Church of God in Christ (COGIC) and namesake of the Bishop Ford Freeway. The list includes a Who's Who of Chicago personalities, athletes, businessmen, and entertainers, including Olympic sprinter Jesse Owens; Adrian "Cap" Anson, Hall of Fame Chicago Cubs player from 1876 to 1897; and Keith Barrow, the son of Reverend Willie Barrow of Operation Push. Barrow was a very popular singer and composer. Others include Enrico Fermi, the Nobel Prize-winning physicist associated with the development of the atomic bomb; Thomas Dorsey, "father of gospel music"; Ida B. Wells, journalist and activist who fought against lynching; Robert Sengstacke Abbott, founder of the *Chicago Defender*; and Roebuck "Pop" Staples of the Staples Singers.

As mentioned earlier, American history and Chicago history are intertwined in the graveyards. During the Civil

Old mausoleum near entrance

War, captured Confederate soldiers were kept in Camp Douglas, which was on land owned by Senator Stephen A. Douglas. Many of these captives died from diseases and from the severe weather conditions. They were originally buried in the City Cemetery, which was located in what is now Lincoln Park. When this land was developed into a park, all of the bodies had to be relocated. The remains of more than 5,000 of these soldiers are buried in Oak Woods. The remaining bodies were moved to Rose Hill and Graceland cemeteries. The gravesites at Oak Woods are marked with a 46-foot-tall monument topped by a statue of a Confederate soldier. Several cannons and cannonballs surround "Confederate Mound."

Three things I learned

Among the people I mentioned who are buried in Oak Woods are many African Americans. Ironically, African-American burials were not officially permitted until 1963 because people not already owning plots could not purchase them.

While reading about the story of Camp Douglas, I learned that an attempted escape by some of the Confederate prisoners was prevented by Allen Pinkerton, who founded the Secret Service. Earlier, Pinkerton had discovered a plot to assassinate President Lincoln.

The monument for the graves of the Confederate soldiers was dedicated in 1895 by President Grover Cleveland.

Bernard C. Turner

Holy Trinity Orthodox Cathedral

Elaborate and ornate interior design.

There are treasures to see in Chicago—treasures of Chicago history and treasures of Chicago's diverse communities. There is no better example of Chicago's hidden treasures than Louis Sullivan's Holy Trinity Orthodox Cathedral, built in 1903. The cathedral is located northwest of the Loop at 1121 North Leavitt Street in what is now Ukrainian Village.

Yes, it's true: This great Chicago architect designed a Russian Orthodox cathedral, and he incorporated many elements of traditional Russian-Byzantine style into the work. Sullivan hoped that Holy Trinity would be one of the most unique and poetic buildings in the country. When you visit this church—and note that I am saying "when," not "if"—you will agree that the building has fulfilled his wish.

Like so many Chicago stories, this one begins at the World's Columbian Exposition. The Russian presence at the Exposition included a bell that was intended to be used after the Exposition for a grand church to be built for the small but growing Russian community in Chicago. In 1892, a parish was formed and a church was built on North Racine Avenue. Incidentally, the Russian bell is on the list of items missing from the Columbian Exposition: It was stolen from the church. (I have discovered during my time as president of the Chicago History Museum that there

is no end to the artifacts from that exposition that are either missing or that one community or another believes should be moved back to a proper place in Chicago!)

The pastor of Holy Trinity, Reverend John Kochurov, chose Louis Sullivan for the important assignment of designing a new church. The design chosen was that of a modest Russian provincial church, rather than something grander, along the lines of a Moscow or St. Petersburg church. Parishioners, "who were country people who had come from southern Russia near the Ukraine and the area around the Carpathian Mountains"[1], welcomed this idea.

The church was begun with a gift of $4,000 from Czar Nicholas II. As you may

Square bell tower with octagonal belfry.

know, that was the Czar who, along with his family, was killed by the Bolsheviks. Czar Nicholas is now a saint of the Russian Orthodox Church. Reverend Kochurov eventually went back to Russia, where, on

Ceiling with icons of saints.

What makes the exterior of the church startling is the knowledge that Louis Sullivan designed it. At 47 x 98 feet, it is smaller than some of the other churches in Ukrainian Village. The square bell tower, with its octagonal belfry, dominates the scene. Upon closer examination, it is apparent that the exterior trim is metal, not wood. This is not only consistent with churches in Russia but also suggestive of trades engaged in by Holy Trinity's parishioners in Chicago. You can see that, unlike most Western churches, the body of the church is square and that the dome is octagonal. That shape, rather than any decoration, arouses curiosity about what is inside.

The interior is elaborate. The dome soars above the parishioners who gather for the sung liturgy. There are some features of Sullivan's design that are reminiscent of Pilgrim Baptist Church, the Adler and Sullivan creation that, tragically, burned in January 2006. These features include soaring heights and an interior molded by complex alignments, rather than by 90-degree angles. Light pours in from above. Notice the attention to wood, one of Sullivan's hallmarks, including the oversized capitals on the pillars and the beadwork that breaks up the long lines of the wood.

There are also icons of saints that are of particular significance in the Orthodox tradition. One of them is dedicated to St. John Kochurov. There is a large central figure of the saint, surrounded by eleven scenes from his life. Look carefully

October 31, 1917[2], he also was killed by the Bolsheviks. In 1994, he was glorified as a saint. So Chicago can claim its own saint, and Holy Trinity owes its existence to two Russian Orthodox saints[3].

at the figure depicted in a panel on the left side. Find the man in the business suit. That's our own Louis Sullivan! You will see that Sullivan has handed the plans of the church to St. John Kochurov. Kochurov has a halo; Sullivan does not. Perhaps Sullivan was not a saint, but now he is a presence in Chicago's iconography.

Look at the other panels, and you will learn more about St. John Kochurov—his birth and youth in Russia, his years in America, and his return to the Soviet Union, where "in 1917 he becomes the first martyr among the clergy under the godless powers."

In the background of the panel showing the saint overseeing the religious education of children, there is a view of the church's Chicago neighborhood. The tower of Sullivan's church transforms the scene into one that would easily fit into a view of Russia itself. Although it is idealized, this view sheds light on the project that Sullivan undertook, and on the hopes and dreams that Chicago's Russian community had for this church when the building was first commissioned.

As you leave Holy Trinity, cross to the west side of Leavitt and look back toward the church and toward the city in the background. This is the view depicted in the icon. I am sure that you will share the gratitude that I feel every time I stand there after a visit: gratitude for a community that wanted to leave its mark on the city, gratitude for a pastor who had the courage to make this project come to life, and gratitude to a great architect who was willing to challenge himself to do something very unusual at a point late in his career— design a Russian church.

These days, the church is open mainly on Saturday afternoons, but if you would like to visit at another time, please call the church. My experience is that they will be happy to make special arrangements for you. The telephone number is (773) 486-6064. The church sometimes has docent-led visits. When you are there, ask the docents if they will let you climb to the top of the bell tower!

Gary T. Johnson
President, Chicago
History Museum

[1] George A. Lane, S.J., *Chicago Area Churches and Synagogues: An Architectural Pilgrimage*. Loyola University Press, Chicago, Ill. 1981. Page 106. This is a wonderful reference for church treasures in Chicago.
[2] http://www.oca.org/FS.NA-Saint.asp?SID=4&Saint=John
[3] *The Orthodox Church in America*, "St. John Kochurov, Missionary to America and First Hieromartyr under the Bolshevik Yoke." http://www.oca.org/FS.NA-Saint.asp?SID=4&Saint=John

Photo Credits

Alfred Caldwell Lily Pool
Bronzeville
Bud Billiken Day Parade
Chicago Temple
Dawes House
DuSable Museum of African-American History
Gold Coast
Green Line 'L' West
Lincoln Park (Neighborhood)
Marshall Field's
Mexican Fine Arts Center Museum
Oak Woods Cemetery
All photos by Bernard C. Turner

Chicago Cultural Center
Exterior photos by Bernard C. Turner
Tiffany dome photo by Hedrich Blessing

Charnley-Persky House Museum
Interior photo by Hedrich Blessing, Courtesy of Skidmore,
Owings, & Merrill
Exterior photos by Donald Kalec, courtesy of the Charnley-
Persky House Museum

Chinese-American Museum of Chicago
Chinese-American Museum garment photo courtesy of Sheila
Chin
Chinatown photos by Bernard C. Turner

Civic Opera House
Photos courtesy of Dan Rest and Cheri Eisenberg

Clarke House Museum
Clarke House exterior photo by Michael Beasley, courtesy of the
Chicago Department of Cultural Affairs
Dining Room and Parlor photos by Peter J. Schultz, courtesy of
the Chicago Department of Cultural Affairs

Downtown River Walk
Graceland Cemetery
Green Line 'L' South
Brown Line 'L' South
Haymarket Square
Holy Family Church
Lincoln Park (Park)
Moody Bible Institute and Church
All photos by Greg Borzo

Featured Entry:
Holy Trinity Orthodox Cathedral
Photos by Gary Johnson,
President, Chicago History Museum

Front cover
Clarke House exterior photo by Michael Beasley, courtesy of the
Chicago Department of Cultural Affairs
Standing Lincoln in Lincoln Park photo by Greg Borzo

Back cover
Lincoln Square photo by Bernard C. Turner

Bibliography

Danckers, Ulrich, and Meredith, Jane. *Early Chicago*. River
Forest, Ill.: Early Chicago Inc., 2000.

Grossman, James R., Keating, Ann Durkin, and Reiff, Janice L.,
Editors. *Encyclopedia of Chicago*. Chicago and London:
University of Chicago Press, 2004.

Longstreth, Richard, Editor. *The Charnley House*. Chicago:
University of Chicago Press, 2004.

Hayner, Don, and McNamee, Tom. *Streetwise Chicago: A History of
Chicago Street Names*. Chicago: Loyola University Press, 1998.

Miller, Donald. *City of the Century*. New York: Touchstone, 1997.

Moffat, Bruce. *The 'L': The Development of Chicago's Rapid Transit
System, 1888-1932*. Chicago: Central Electric Railfans' Assn.,
1995.

Pacyga, Dominic. *Chicago, City of Neighborhoods*. Chicago: Loyola
University Press, 1986.

Sinkevitch, Alice, Editor. *AIA Guide to Chicago*. Orlando, Fla.:
Harcourt, 2004.

park. He also provides Green Line and Brown Line 'L' tours and guided tours of Bronzeville.

In 2002, Mr. Turner founded Highlights of Chicago Press with the publication of *A View of Bronzeville*, a neighborhood tour guide that focuses on the important institutions and people that made Bronzeville a great neighborhood. The second publication, *TJ and the Mysterious Stranger*, is a children's story that also gives the history of the Bud Billiken character. And most recently there is a new social studies book for elementary children called, *Our Chicago—People and Places*.

Mr. Turner is available to speak to audiences, school groups and to conduct tours. He especially likes working with teachers and children to discuss Chicago history and culture with a highlight on Chicago neighborhoods, yesterday and today.

Bernard C. Turner

Bernard Turner was born in Bronzeville and educated in the Chicago Public School system. He studied German as an undergraduate at University of Illinois, Urbana-Champaign and attended graduate school at the University of Chicago. Mr. Turner has been a teacher of German and Spanish on the secondary level and has worked in educational publishing in sales and marketing since 1978. Currently, he is a district sales manager for Zaner-Bloser Educational Publishers and a docent at the Chicago History Museum. He gives tours on Chicago history at CHM, and walking tours of Old Town and Lincoln Park, the

Suzanne Haynes

Suzanne Haynes was born and raised in northeast Montana but has lived in seven major U.S. cities, Chicago being her favorite. She graduated from Northwestern University with a degree in literature and is retired after working 30 years for the U.S. Railroad Retirement Board. Suzanne gives tours for the Chicago History Museum and volunteers for The Chicago Humanities Festival and the Lincoln Park Zoo. She has traveled throughout the Americas, Western Europe and the Near East. While only living in Chicago for 15 years, Suzanne believes you can see greatness better when you have a lot to compare it to.

Greg Borzo

Greg Borzo was born in Ravenswood and has lived in Chicago most
of his life. With a Master's Degree in journalism from Northwestern
University, he has worked most of his career as a journalist. He was
Midwest Bureau Chief for *Traffic World* and Editor-in-Chief of *Modern
Railroads*. After turning to health and science writing, he became the
Health and Science Editor at *American Medical News,* the weekly
newspaper of the American Medical Association. He is currently Media
Manager for Science at The Field Museum.

Borzo has won many awards, including two Peter Lisagor Awards from
the Chicago Chapter of the Society of Professional Journalists and two
Golden Trumpets from the Publicity Club of Chicago. An avid bicyclist
and movie fan, he reviews bike movies for the Chicagoland Bicycle
Federation.

Borzo pursues history as a hobby. At the Chicago History Museum,
he leads tours of the Brown and Green elevated rail lines as well as
Lincoln Park.